MW01228615

The War's Kite And The Immigration's Key:
"Her Name is Muhammad"

Second Edition
Language: English
Dimensions: 6 x 0.42 x 9 inches

The War's Kite And The Immigration's Key:

"Her Name is Muhammad"

Lama Muhammad. MD

To all minds and souls who suffered occult or overt prejudice:

Never Give Up!

You are in another world, the ocean of charming Magic Realism, and every resemblance to reality in names, events, or places is purely coincidental.
Don't you believe in "chance"?

1-Virtual Diary

I'm still sewing in swans' jackets ‹nor do I give up, and the curse is not too.
What increases the pain of spinning is that the threads are made of nettles, the nettles of the torment of youth, the screechy voices of mothers, and the crying sounds of lovers and children.
And everything that passes unnoticed during the era of globalization due to the noise of absurdity, imitation, and consumption.
I spin jackets out of the whole truth, and the truth, if it is complete, it hurts all sides, and everyone hates it.
 Only God guarantees her survival and passage from one generation to the next.
All the half-truths are gathered here, regardless of each party's attempt to bring me wool from their own city only; others get cotton from their borders, a thread from the sadness of her relatives, and a rag from the frameworks of specific beliefs.
What makes this jacket magical is that it speaks for everyone. Each party has a half-truth that tells the story of its place of origin.
Each party thinks it is entirely right and neglects the rest of the parties.
No one likes a jacket of nettles' truth.
As in myths, I must be silent and not waste time on hollow justifications as I spin this book:
The justifications filled the opponents' words when they stood against the loyalists' right to the homeland and life.
The justifications color the loyalists' statements when they object to the opposition's rights in the homeland and life.
I do not have the right to cry, scream, collapse, or surrender.
Alone here, shunned with my truth in a time of civil war and politics shrouded in religion.
****

Since he traveled to Syria, nothing remains of Ali except the scraps of his conversation papers.

I wrote it in my handwriting to repeat it with all my senses, not just my eyes, then spread it all over the apartment.

I treated them as a lucky amulet, or perhaps they were the only witness to my sorrow and the fragments of my heart scattered between East and West.

All I know is the Syrian entered territory from the north; that was his last message.

I tried a lot to ask people about northern Syria, its conditions, and its security; I heard five different answers.

Oh God, how can we not know what is really happening in the time of globalization, television, and internet?

How do they sew billions of these half-truths to hold people accountable?

My illness, like any autoimmune disease, flares up with my sadness.

The talk of Syria or Iraq and its burning in my heart has never been more painful than these days.

Many have tried to find out why I care so much about Iraq. I am Damascene by birthplace.

It has long stories, not the first I lived in Iraq for years because of my family's work there.

Not the least of them is the Iraqi family that helped us one day in Algeria when my father worked there for two years.

However, the most important is my prophecy that Iraq is the origin of all middle eastern countries and the beginning of the map of the world.

Ali also has a significant share in the stories of Iraq's love.

He told me many tails about its history and the unique stories from its feasts and funerals.

He worked there for several years and accompanied Hamza.

Hamza is an Iraqi whose mother's lineage returns to Ahl al-Bayt*.

His family is of great importance in Iraq. He mediated one day to pardon an apostate person and secured an entry visa for that person to Sweden.

When he told me that story last year, I was astonished:

-Apostate? How did they know about his religion?

-One of the beneficiaries fabricated the accusation against him because he tried to fight his corruption.

- For God's sake, are you serious?

-Yes. The prevailing culture in Iraq now, which strict religious parties supported, is the legislation of atonement and allowing the ignorant who do not decipher the meaning of a statement to control the fates of the brains that want reform and better changes.

Hamza knew that, and with his lineage influence, he could help.

-How many people have no Hamza? How can anyone dare speak on God's behalf and throw the robes of faith at whomever he wants.

-All our countries need the separation of religion from civil society and law, the differentiation between mosques and universities.

-My Jewish grandmother used to say: Don't put your nose in others' beds or prayers!

-I can't agree more.

If Iraq is liberated and stands up again, all middle eastern countries will have an open horizon.

Thus, Iraq remained in my prayers with Syria and any suffering area in this wild world.

I experienced the similarities between people in stories and revolutions, and my sadness doubled.

I grieved for developing countries while their land is a mine of riches and authentic and ancient peoples are estranged like gypsies searching for dignified lives. Sadness has refined me to a level of courage that entered my dreams and filled my will with hope.

You know that your brain and conscience guide you, not your grudges or tradition when you support the oppressed in your region, your country, a strange country, and an "enemy" country.

Support justice means helping the oppressed in any part of the earth. Humanity is indivisible; it does not recognize the limits of geography nor the lies of history.

And for today's virtual space prayer:

If God sees you, why do you need people?

They took advantage of your work; no problem, your deed is in the world's energy.

They called you what you are not; no big deal, believe in Karma.

It doesn't matter who got offended by your kindness, nor who stabbed your back.

Thank those who stabbed back and made God your helper.

May we get more back wounds, not hearts.

****

I put all my clothes aside. A mountain of black calmness rolled into the corner; no color speaks louder than black and no more beautiful than it. I love the beauty of our peels, "clothes, jackets, and fabrics," but I don't care about the so-called brands or the ridiculousness of distinctive, unrefined dresses.

How can a sane person take care of letters on his jacket while semi-naked children die every minute of their need for bread?

The middle class I grew up in taught me that a person gives value to things, from the name to a car, and not the opposite.

Nothing is worse than waiting for someone's shoes to give him a "value."

I was cleaning the place while contemplating this world.

-Oh, Alia..Dr. Muhammad, can you give up on the mission impossible of changing this world?

Then started to sort clothes according to their rituals.

Today and in the new era in which I can buy what I want, I don't care what I wear, but I care about how my health is?

Before the brand of my bag come the simplicity and elegance of my appearance.

My favorite questions became:

- Before measuring my waist: Did I allow fat to eat my arteries?

-Did I allow a lack of sleep to plow my face? Can I answer before putting on makeup?

I tried to strengthen myself more, so I resorted to helping more patients. I took over an extra work of a colleague, who was overwhelmingly trying to get pregnant through IVF. I excellently finished her work above mine. In addition, I started teaching at the university for medical students.

I started new sessions for residents, "cinema-therapy": Teaching psychotherapy through movies. We discussed the art of psychoanalysis, nonverbal communication, and the body language of the film's heroes. Also, we discussed the diagnosis of personality disorders and learned about fascinating attachment theories.

I responded to the pending friendship requests, perhaps carrying news from the Levant.

I turned my Facebook into a diary and put all the places I visit, museums, gardens, cultural landmarks, restaurants, and artistic and literary events daily with my opinion about things.

I made all the above under the rule of absolute privacy; there is no need for our homes to remain open doors, even if they are virtual.

Making your Facebook into a diary, so most events and coordinates are shared with you, helps keep your memories and assure your thoughtfulness.

Not only because some are hungry while you are eating in the most famous restaurant, but also out of respect for people's time and trying not to waste it pursuing the absurdities of a life that belongs to you only.

After telling them their duty to bear sadness in my weather, I spent my vacation with my friends. They did, and I loved them more. Sharing sorrow -not joy- makes excellent friendship.

I am thinking of changing this tiny apartment. I want to buy a house.

In the United States of America, you buy everything in convenient installments if you have a good "credit score," which signifies your sincerity and commitment to paying your debts.

While getting ready to make evening tea, I continued to wash every single thought of mine and put her in my goals' space to dry.

Buying a small house will give me a kind of warmth, mainly if I paint it with my hands and make its small details match my tiny wishes. It will ease - perhaps - my thinking about peace and war.

I put a cup of green matcha tea in front of me on the desk. This type of tea has countless benefits. I don't know why we don't grow it in the Middle East.

Once again, you are thinking of the Middle East; Alia, the queen of persistence!

I start knitting a new sweater with the scent of matcha, smiling; the middle eastern storyteller has no place in the Levant countries and looking for a small house in beautiful America.

2- Baghdad

It sounds like
Your love is like the sun in a snowy land
And the hope is so great that you will never leave
The darkness is getting stronger
It calls for your presence
You are today just as you were yesterday:
Warmth, shadows, and hymns of a human resurrection
At a time when faith became a sin
Tell me, by your Lord, isn't "God" more significant than anyone?
Tell your children about me
Teach them that the "Earth" rotates
Just like time
And death is spinning
Just like the earth
And we are as we are
We deny the dizziness sound and reject the voice of love
****

Heba and Ammar's relationship is still dancing like a candle lighting the place, but there is no hope for its eternal continuation.

-I heard the Friday sermon from the ignorant and illiterate Sheik who took over the mosque across from my friend's house, so the place turned from a house of worship to a house of hate. Hatred for all people other than his flocks.

We have the five pillars of fake Islamization:

- Revenge and sectarian retaliation.
- Female infanticide under the Niqab and confiscation of women's human rights.
- Idol worship, the idols of tradition, the immorality of the inheritance.
- Maids and enslaved people.

21

- Many Gods: Watch beards and crowns compete for God's place in washed minds.
Which religion is this distorted by the tongues and heads of its followers?
Fake Islamization is their new religion, and Muslims are paying the price.
-Who told you we would be silent?
****

No place had love in my heart as the lady of the sites: "Baghdad."
She has the stubbornness to be rebellious in the face of foolish politicians and oil and religious traders.
The "shrewd" merchants bought places and attributed them to God. Then robbed the poor to clad the stones; they raped women with forced marriage contracts and adultery.
The boys inherited oil and gas, and instead of making their countries like Dubai, they allowed illiterate beards to control people in the streets.
They released the hands of criminals in the name of religion and contributed to spreading global terror from "Islam." What horror is more significant than ahead infested with sex?
-What does sex-infested mean?
- What do you expect from someone who blows himself up in the hope of the Paradise of Al-Hoor Al-Ain?
What do you expect from one who considers women sexual pleasure?
-Sex is a necessary human need; they have no shame if they think about it.
-Seriously! Humanity elevates sex so that man becomes distinct from animals, just as it promotes the mind, so sex becomes a means, not a purpose. When sex becomes a purpose - even in relationships - the relationship ends unhumanly.
- Possible. Relationships that kill love spread with hateful words that we heard today from that Sheik. Some good Sheiks raise their heads out there. Those who tell you, for example, that religion is how you treat others. They stand as good examples with their honesty and genuine peaceful intentions.

-Maybe it's my misfortune, but I haven't met anyone yet. Everyone I met asked me about my hair before work and the treatment of people; what can I do? No worries, I hope you are right.

Ammar's long discussions with Heba increased his love and fear for her. While he was trying hard to protect her and make her see him, she was trying to save the world.

Abeer still has a beautiful effect on his soul, but he is " eastern" enough to fall in love with a lady that doesn't see him.

He is the one who lived to live and life in his view: "To secure a house, a car, and money, to live in dignity and the noble goal is a success."

Shocked by a woman who sees life: "Help others, brave opinions, saving humanity, and the noblest goal is immortality."

They walked for a long time through the sad streets of Baghdad. Then she said goodbye:

- I have to buy some food and go home, see you tomorrow.

He did not say to her, " take me with you," as he thought; instead, he said: -Take care of yourself.

He turned his back before she left. He was always afraid she would turn her back one day, forever. So maybe that's why he goes just by her hinting at leaving.

He walked for a long time in the streets of Baghdad. He passed by the most famous restaurant and carts of boiled corn, luxury cars, and barefoot children.

He passed through elaborate mosques and houses without windows.

He passed by women with Niqab; he did not know if they were males or females.

He passed by a child with torn clothes wiping shoes with the horror of the whole world in her eyes. Then he saw a teenager driving a car with a government number, screaming at the (pain) of the traffic policeman.

Ammar passed through Baghdad with her broken hope, drenched with the urine of officials before the rain of God, and when his mind could not bear more pain, he sat on one of the cracked street benches contemplating the sky.

-Iraq into revolution; I almost swear about this.

At least a night like this without bombings is like our dream of safety.

As for Heba, she returned to the room she called home to find a message on her door. It was not similar to the threatening letters she receives every day. She thought:

Should I open it? Perhaps it contains "anthrax" and maybe another death, "Shall I open it?"

****

Death raises its head from the witnessing alleys; its tails follow in whirlpools that suffocate children and dreams.

-These bastards who burned the country were not from the space; they were citizens who caused this madness.

-I try a lot to put justifications for people, but what justifies extremism?! Nothing justifies seeing blood within a sect!

Poverty has become the master of the situation, and looting is still ongoing. They are not ashamed; they are not ashamed!

Death was a new friend I bargain him every morning; I looked in his eyes and begged him:

Do you accept sacrifice? What we heard in legends and tales about kings and gods who received sacrifices is true?

If you are the angel of death, what is wrong with you? Go away, take the Sultans, Kings, the oil traders, and the women abusers.

What's wrong with you? Why do you go after the good guys?

Lebanon was a second home for Abeer despite the snub of sectarians and haters.

She made many friends, but Ella had a beautiful space in her heart.

Ella, the Lebanese journalist, resembles Beirut in her honesty, beauty, and kindness. She found Abeer crying on the university's runway after a lecture on the (Arab Spring).

After a long conversation, she offered Abeer to rent a room in her house for half the price of the cold basement that Abeer had rented before.

Abeer accepted without reservations; souls sometimes meet before their bodies.

Abeer did not find a job as a nurse. She currently works as a waitress in a local restaurant. She was still going around universities and cultural centers to hear lectures about her country. Yet, at the same time, she saw hungry children in the streets wiping shoes and car windows belonging to rich people; she knew that some of " the rich" contributed in one way or another to the lectures and the continuation of the farce.

Abeer was still loyal to the poor, seeing them in all their colors and positions, not only the poor who belong to the same sect by sexual coincidences.

The Syrian opposition - in most of them - closed their eyes from seeing injustice if it was in the hands of those who fight the regime. As a result, the crimes committed by factions affiliated with the Syrian revolution have disappeared from the human rights manuscripts claimed by the opposition.

The book is still her good friend, and she is still a "book's mouse."

After one of the funded lectures, she came out angry. She saw nothing from the place, but memories of a quiet Syrian morning filled with the smell of thyme and coffee. The voice of Fairuz singing, "Y' Jabal Albaeed." *

On a stone bench, she opened a book by Tolstoy and began to read.

-You read a lot. Do you write?

-No, I just read and think.

-I did not adopt the fashion of writing too; that became everyone's job in the virtual time, while scarcity does read.

From the heart of the distant mountain of Fairuz:

The soul smiled using the man's body in front of her.

 A young Lebanese man names Diyar.

The mother of Diyar had Syrian roots; she met his Lebanese father, Alam, in Iraq - when they worked in their countries' embassies - and then moved with him to Lebanon. She gave birth to Diyar before breast cancer attacked her. She told Alam:

-Get married, that's your right. I am dying.

And he answered:

-Do you see me as a jerk, dear? You are on one side of my life scale and the whole world on the other.

Ironically, Diyar's father died of myocardial infarction, and his mother survived ten years after him.

When she passed away, the name Alam was her last word.

Diyar was left alone between his mother's family in Syria and his father's family in Lebanon.

It was strange for Diyar to tell this story to Abeer in their first meeting. She smiled and said to herself:

-A rare kind man.

And he saw the Syrian scent of his mother and his father's sincerity in her eyes.

****

Facebook has become a bleak place full of pictures of weddings and navigator nights, full of jealousy, hidden hatred with sectarianism, with absurdity.

The ego appears between the lines and in immature reactions.

The majority mastered acting and swam with the current of dragging the herd. Whoever used their brains or left the herd paid the price in a hurricane in his virtual house; however, he lived in the rare case of self-honesty!

Honesty pushes you to see your negatives before your positives, accepting the positives of others and overlooking their negatives.

Honesty encapsulates humility and the actual knowledge that we are all food for earthworms.

Thus, Facebook no longer tempts me to see people discussing half-lives and half-truths. Instead, it has become a means that serves one purpose: To win the enmities of narcissists and the hearts of kind people.

It was a step to combat a threatening depression stalking me since I traveled. So, I opened my Facebook door for the first time in a long time and wrote:

"The truth resides in the bodies of the dead.

 And the dead bodies are contained in the dust of any place.

Life taught me to be humble as dust; the humbler you are, the closer you get to the truth".

The first comment and the first "like" encouraged me, but the first post that made me happy was from "Raafat Tamim" who is this?

A young Jordanian man. His page indicates that he is a well-educated person. His quotations are primarily from dissident Arab writers, many of them are in the diaspora.

There is a strangeness of one color in his virtual house, a strangeness that you feel that the place is not his; like the houses of someone who rents furniture, he does not put his touch on the house, nor does he tell people about his "truth."

I remembered after that that I had to pay my apartment rent, so I went to another website.

-Yogurt for dinner!

My diet includes many vegetables, fruits, eggs, milk, and yogurt. The taste of sugar that I forgot no longer tempts me, but on the contrary, I feel it is as heavy on my stomach as expatriation.

I still write stories and novels; my path seems full of obstacles as long as I don't party and unless I applaud for this and that.

Ahlam sent me a message:

-What's up?

-One Arabic publishing house betrayed my trust; it did not announce the book as it should or distribute it fairly. Another publisher told me: They were afraid of publishing and distributing the book as it should cross the red lines, and they were afraid to tell me about this so that I would reveal the hidden in the virtual space.

-Why don't you write everyday things? Why are you not proud of their victories? Ahlam sent with a smiley face.

-Right, they asked me about this too. I told them it is challenging to write about ordinary things, as our lives are full of explosives and fateful issues.

-You are wiser than expected. How do we learn the art of hypocrisy or what is professionally called: Diplomacy?

-The first time I wanted to be a diplomat was when a writer requested my opinion about his article; he wrote proudly about his Arab lineage. I told him that although we should be proud of our different selves, we must try to change the present and improve the future of developing countries. He replied that I should keep the "correct" opinions to myself.

Why can we not accept the full images but always go too far in our reactions?

-They are the children of the flood, so how can they know about the tides?

-Yes, he changed the subject to tell me about our wars and conquests' victories. Can you imagine how the meeting ended?

I gave up my budding diplomacy and flapped my wings in his face.

-I expected, although you are wise and calm, you know precisely when to brave.

-Thanks, wars cannot bear the word "victory" except in the dictionary of the beneficiaries. No sane person believes in victory when mothers have lost their children; children have lost their feet, and the men of the earth have been humiliated by "testosterone's males."

-Agreed. Whoever starts a war will lose it; whoever participates in it will be bitten or gnawed from the face of his humanity.

-Jealousy and ignorance nibble the poor ego, so they turn into trumpets: with or against. Both sides are, in one or another way, "East."

-They are loyal to people, not to ideas or a country.

They embrace disparaging people, not vilifying ideas - there is no difference.

-In both cases, we are talking about the ego's fragility, not the mind's stability.

-Blessed who used his mind in the era of the new religion!

- I love our "diplomacy," even if it hinders our fame and ambition in the writing world.

-I love you too, sis.

Ahlam is a beautiful brown Yemeni woman like Yemen in beauty and sanity.

Ahlam is the queen of planning; the best person to prepare for projects.

Luck did not enter her dictionary, not by mistake nor by chance.

In short, coincidences did not come close to Ahlam as the orchestrated things approached her.

When she decided to work, she taught Arabic literature for a year and learned UpToDate things in the art of education.

Then she interviewed at all the private schools in the region.

She did not find a job because what the West calls favoritism, and the East calls mediation, did not exist in her life.

She started giving private lessons in the Arabic language and lived a boring life until she decided to change.

And change for the hardworking often requires effort, so she started interpreting the Qur'an.

Every week she interprets a verse based on the origins and rules of the Arabic language.

She started with the Quranic verse:

"Invite to Lord's Way with wisdom and good advice, and debate with them in the most dignified manner.".

And she explained:

No one has the right to invite people to enter his religion. However, with knowledge and morals, he can set an example for anyone on this earth.

This is how you give the right impression about your religion.

As for those who degrade you and insult you, use wisdom to discuss any disagreement.

Wisdom is the head of any religion.

Ahlam continued to do this until the extremists shed her blood.

And the Hareem* attacked her: "You are a woman who does not have the right to speak about religion." The males defamed her: "Stupid woman who seeks fame."

At that time, Ahlam began the journey of searching for a homeland among the embassies of the West.

In her mind, the Prophet Ibrahim is saying: They did it to me; you know what ignorance and muzzling of the mind can do.

In her heart, Jesus says: They crucified me, and I forgave them.

And in her conscience, the Prophet Muhammad was: Thank you, Ahlam, because you protect me from the repeated distortion of my image and my transformation into another person.

Ahlam emigrated and entered America in 2014; life in America allows freedom of expression to a better extent.

 She contacted me for the first time, and the topic was more than just an introduction; It was a friendship proposal.

-Do you know that we take advantage of those who stab us in the back?

I smiled and said to myself:

Here is another soul that believes that life is all karma:

"So, whosoever does good equal to the weight of an atom, shall see it. And whosoever does evil equal to the weight of an atom, shall see it.".

I wrote to her:

-You can't imagine how much I know this. How about we have coffee together this evening?

 I closed the door of my heart a long time ago and despaired the return of absent brains, but my dreams with Ahlam have another life.

3- Hope Does Not Live in Straw

- I decided to go back before theorizing about the loyalists and opponents. Who knows, if I were in their place, I would have said more than they did. But, gray par excellence, I am!

Who am I to distribute humanity in the Arabic language with Western cups?

"Syria" seemed far away and on fire. Like a piece of another planet announced she would not prostrate to the God of war. Yet, the latter expelled her from his kingdom.

He threw her into the world's hottest and most beautiful region, where all nationalities, sects, and religions gather. Each one believes in a different war god.

God of love distributed hope in bowls of straw to the homes of widows, bereaved, lovers without eyes, and children without legs.

And after he left, everyone discovered that hope does not live in straws and that it only catches love.

I decided to carry the rock of my truth and ascend the past step by step; this is how I know how the war began and how humanity will determine the future of the Gods.

There was a quarter of an hour left for dinner with my friend, Umniah, but she began to hurry me:

-The couscous will get cold. I also made the Algerian Maqroud for you.

-What is the Algerian Maqroud?

-Dessert with semolina and dates; from our culture, my beautiful Algerian grandmother taught me to make good dishes and sweets that build happiness.

-Is it not enough for you that I ignored my diet, you also want me to try sugar after boycotting it for months?

-Good food ignites the fire of hope and kneads happiness. So how do you live without sugar? Your heart is so powerful!

Noble Umniah, with her friendship and sincerity, deserves not only that my diet fails again. But also, to think about her point of view on food.

As a doctor, I used to hear doctors' advice about diet, but I never listened to any of them talk about the role of happiness in the metabolism of food.

Perhaps this is an excuse to go back to bad eating habits, and maybe it is a reality that supports her viewpoint in the world of spirituality.

Hawariya was Umniah's paternal grandmother; she was born in Saudi Arabia to Algerian parents who worked there.

They had Amina - the mother of Umniah - who married another noble Saudi man and gave birth to Umniah and Amin.

Amin died in a terrible car accident with his mother on a black night. Ten-year-old Umniah stayed with her Algerian grandmother Hawariya after that.

She learned to cook Algerian dishes and experienced the customs of Algeria; the country became a big part of her heart, even though she had never visited it.

When Umniah married, her husband was entirely unlike her father and grandfather. So, she lived the meaning of true orphanhood in the hands of that puritanical traitor.

When she moved with him to work in America, she knew that she could say no, recognized the meaning of being respected, and started thinking differently.

Her presence in my life gave me the warmth of the family. She treated me like her sister; she was the bond and the sanctuary while trying with the kindness of a holy spirit and the cunning of a wounded woman to get a divorce from a reckless male.

She kept my secrets and overlooked my lapses; she always interpreted my kindness positively, so how could I not neglect my diet and adopt the recipe of her happy Algerian Maqroud!

****

-Why do we need the time? I don't care how much time I spend in Lebanon; I feel it is another life passed while here.

Most people here are kind, but like any place on earth, some are assholes, ignorant, and hateful, nonverbal racism shines with stinginess and meanness's eyes.

Unfortunately, everything you heard here about people who beat Syrian children and took advantage of poor young women is true.

As the more remarkable aspect is luminous, the majority helped without waiting for anything in return. The majority has not forgotten the pain of the Lebanese civil war nor the green cedar of generosity that symbolizes the jewel of the east, Lebanon.

- When will you return to Syria, Abeer?

- I don't know, I'm afraid!

- Afraid? of whom?

- From all sides. In Syria, parties differ in their names, but the consequences on kind people are the same.

- Do you still support the theory of the third party that killed the demonstrators in Syria?

- Perhaps, Ella. I have reached the stage of questioning everything; I do not know the truth except that everyone - without exception - drank from the cup of humiliation and death. What do you think?

- My opinion is simple and naive. The third party in any relationship is in close contact with one of the two parties; also, one of these original parties supports it. This is logical and happens even in marital infidelities.

As well we can see it when the boss-subordinate has an intimate relationship. And in the suppression of revolutions by the regimes using a third party.

- What if there is a beneficiary from continuing the war between the two parties? Who is using a third party, then?

In this case, the party with authority must withdraw in recognition of its negligence and allow the idea of the third party first.

And to spare the bloodshed and cut off the road to the beneficiaries second. This is what history calls: political astuteness or honorable stance.

-What do you call what happened in Syria?

-Some call it a revolution; others call it a crisis, a civil war, a regional war, a war against terrorism, a desire for a coup, or a sectarian war. War by proxy: the war between Saudi Arabia and Iran, the battle of America and Russia.

The result is the same: a country was destroyed with the participation of all without exception.

- What do you call it, Abeer?

-Look, Ella, my answer is all the above:

One party wanted a revolution:

They wanted to stand in the bread queue in the morning with the poor and the rich, the official and the political prisoner.

They wanted good differentiation between the good and the bribed, the writers and the political analysts.

They wished for a homeland that can have us all, educated and the fawning, the prostitutes and the Sheikhs, the strong woman and the Hareem*, the men and the males.

Many parties are involved in this "revolution" as well, with many motives.

Some wanted revenge, "the spiteful"; some wished to serve the present as " they don't care," becoming the war's kings. Some wanted to build a better future for their grandchildren because they "have a dream."

We heard a lot of statements. Everyone supports their party:

So many parties said Syria, Israel's neighbor, has a ceiling of development that it could not overcome. And when it arrived, the traitors brought it back to zero.

The oil and gas countries and the countries of the West have some terrorists that must act in some way; Open the door of "jihad" in Syria, and we will get rid of them.

A country of mosaics, you want it Sunni, you want it Shiite, pay for guns and sedition.

The war of the major powers in this century is more dangerous than taking place on their soil. Syria is a place for World War III.

People are accustomed to worshiping idols and breaking them as well.

-Let them pay the price for the sweat of the poor in all the Arab countries and make it a bad example.

Millions of the bastards of the wealthy Arabs will lose if the crows disagree on destroying the country.

An Islamic caliphate ruled by the ignorant.

No to the rule of minorities that allow you to worship whoever you want.

What is better to fast and pray with clogs of extremities dictatorship or get the change through military boots?

Oh, dear Ella, the issue is more complex than what one party wanted by himself or what a good or a wrong person thinks; the conflict is to continue for years, needs firewood from the heart of the country, and sparks to ignite from the outside, no need for more than volunteers to exporting sparks.

You told me that you read the myths of the struggle of the Greeks Gods! Watch it now, broadcast live and direct.

What has changed is that many people believe in one God now, and we call those who quarrel over thrones kings.

The battles among the kings of sand, the kings of monuments, the kings of oil, the kings of sects, the kings of sex trafficking, the kings of organ trade!

Simple people are the children of these conflicts; they try to survive with a quiet day or some dream, so they leave the homelands; good people like you embrace us and our pain.

Tears pooled in Ella's eyes. This Lebanese woman is much nobler than tolerating all this reality's ugliness.

- It is a farce; its name is a farce, my friend.

The house is your home, Abeer, and I can't imagine my life without you; that's why I ask.

-Leave all this; who will wash the dishes today?

-You, it was my turn yesterday.

- I can't; I must get dressed and meet Diyar.

-Are you kidding me!

-No, why?

-I thought you left him.

-Not yet.

- Oh, mean!

- No, I do not want him to gamble his life with someone like me.

- We went back to the lack of reason. Ok, I will wash the dishes today, and you will do them for two consecutive days, and you will also tell me about Diyar.

-Agreed, Ella, the deer!

-One country, darling.

****

The habit of visiting some fan pages still accompanies me.

It is fun, perhaps, and maybe because Ali was the first to share my stories in the past.

 Nostalgia is overwhelming, and humans are creative in calming the child's anxiety inside them. In every subconscious room lives the child's version of our self and if this kid suffered and didn't get helped, he would never leave you alone.

The first reply to my Facebook post today was from Gaim. And the Gaim name in Arabic means the beautiful fluffy clouds.

Gaim is an old friend born in Morocco to a Moroccan father and a French mother.

He was with me at school. His profile picture on Facebook suggests humility. Brown sandy skin, his eyes are black. It was as if the Amazigh genes wanted nothing but to give him the title of beauty.

He always looks fresh, which speaks of drinking a lot of water and eating vegetables.

I remember the last time I met him and noted the gentle smile on his broad shoulders; he told me that he had finished studying dentistry and would specialize in orthodontics:

"Your cutely misaligned teeth give you unique attraction. Don't consult me.".

He also said that depression killed so many of his dreams that he decided to tackle it with sport:

"A prominent boxer, I do not punch people, but a bag with the word "Depression" written on it, literally!"

Gaim was a dream of love "rain" for many girls from my colleagues, but - as far as I know - he was never in a romantic relationship.

Rumors circulated about his love for a woman ten years older than him. and other stories about the death of his girlfriend in an earthquake in Morocco.

They even questioned his sexual orientation. But Gaim stood on the rumors; he didn't let them burn his educational attainment, nor did he surrender and respond to tongues and talismans.

I told him one day: A psychiatrist is a dentist are best friends.

-How?

- While you want your patient to be silent until you master your work and you talk so that time passes and support the relationship between the doctor and the patient, the opposite happens with us; we are silent most of the time. The patient speaks; this is how we support the therapeutic alliance.

Gaim laughed:

- You mean the dentist is garrulous?

-I don't mean that we complete each other and make friends.

-I am honored to be your friend, Dr.Alia Muhammad.

The important thing is that this Gaim shared my post with the sentence: "God be upon you, Oh Alia, you are still at your principles. Chapeau! A kind word in its simplicity helps to arrange our insides, with all my failures, weakness, and illness.

Gaim's sentence gave me hope today that I had not changed for the worse, as sadness made me think, and I got excited when Ahlam commented:

"Remember Abraham said: "my Lord! Make this city one of peace and security: and preserve my sons and me from worshipping idols."

Then she explained it and added:

Perhaps some people do not imagine that once a worshiper of idols existed. This is what the Qur'an means.

Get out of the herd, and expect your blood is wasted in a country that stabs God and glorifies immature boys.

Then she sent me a private message:

- Alia, I need a brain and a heart to hear me today. Do you accept my invitation?

On a quiet American evening, after another day when people work from 6 to 6. Ahlam and I drink coffee in one of the American (Starbucks) coffee shops.

Ahlam is a tall, slender brunette; her black eyes tell stories. Her Jewish nose made her more attractive and different in the era of similar cosmetic noses.

Starbucks coffee is a chain of coffee shops. Its coffee is unique, and it is not expensive compared to other places.

As you wait for your turn, the Starbucks logo appears: The Two-Tailed Mermaid; the relationship between coffee and sailing is intimate because the relationship between coffee and alienation is intimate.

Starbucks is an American coffee company; Ahlam told me it was started in Washington state years ago by three partners (an English language teacher, writer, and history teacher).

And the name Starbucks came from the character (Starbuck) who loved coffee a lot in the novel (Moby Dick) by American writer Herman Melville.

The novel's events revolved around the dilemma of survival and travel. While a man struggles with a whale in the story, many people work with "whales" in reality.

In summary: Starbucks: Another witness to the American dream, and its ability to succeed, it tells you about the secret of life that lies in:

Continuity: Continuing after failures and disappointments.

Ignoring: ignoring hostility, jealousy, and people's pursuit of their interests.

Independence: financially if you are able, and morally, which is most important.

After Ahlam became financially independent, her ability to defend her rights changed; she sent an invitation to her younger sister in Yemen.

-I am trying to protect her from the oppression of the males in the family. She told me that they were trying to force her to get married. They are males' cousins, not men.

-what are you going to do?

-I'll try to seek her an asylum.

-Sad that we'll continue to seek homelands. Why do we flee from those countries, some of the (wise men) ask.
-What a question, Alia, what a question?

4- I Don't Care If You are Fat or Skinny, I Want You To Be Happy!

It is okay
Y', arrogant of sweet coincidence
I am your rib Eve
Crushed memories
Shaped them as stars
scattered them
Filled the sky of your heart
It is okay
Be proud of your love's victories.
But remember:
How dark are you at my solar eclipse?
I wrote this poem one day for whom I thought it was my first love.
I was young, but the wings of my dreams were more extensive than the
sun. And when that supposed love left me, I imagined that life had
missed its moon. Then I learned that true love does not neglect its
heroes, and a new moon is born as long as you are the sun.
****

After backbiting, how can a "friend" invite you to his house with those
he gossiped about you with them?
How can that hypocrite put your picture with him in a beautiful time?
We know people from their silence and what they do not do more than
what they said or did.
-Why are you nervous, Sanya?
- Remember the candy jug?
- Yes!
- I want one.
- What's the point?

-I want someone to tell me: I don't care if you're fat or skinny; I want you to be happy. I am disappointed with backbiting and gossip.

My weekly call with Sanya has ended; the candy jug has been in its place for years.

There are many meaningful things in my rented apartment; it will not be easy to move them if I buy a house.

I am not one of the people who bring things to their homes for decoration, but rather stuff for remembrance, simple things with stories that bring love to the place or evoke the spirit of passion and the fragrance of a journey!

The candy jug in my apartment has a story unlike any other:

Ghadi* bought it for his girlfriend Sirin, who was a mermaid.

The jug is golden in color; It is transparent, so you can see what is in it.
 It would have been a jug of green matcha tea - as Ghadi wanted it - but Sirin, who has a rare pancreatic disease that makes it necessary for her to eat sweets, made it an antidote to her symptoms filled it with candies and sweets.

Ghadi told her: I don't care. If you are fat or skinny, I want you to be happy! Sirin recovered after that.

From that day, and the jug is for the dessert, the story with her Sirin is a memory.

This is not the whole story, but half of it that the beautiful fifty-year-old star told me, who sat selling (antiques) in Tahrir Square.

She said to me: Take it quickly: "Eighty Egyptian pounds; it doesn't need installment buying.

I saw the magic of Egypt reflected in the golden jug mirror:

The first glory and the first civilization, the first victory and architecture, the first trade, and the first doctor. Egypt, the Nile, the pyramids, the seas and the holy shrines, the tombs of the saints, and the pharaohs.

The beauty of Asia and the attractiveness of Africa, the spirit of Alexander the Great with the heart of Cleopatra. Egypt Ahmed Shawky and Naguib Mahfouz, Umm Kulthum and Abdel Halim. The first story and the first script and dialogue.

The golden jug played in my imagination and showed me Egypt, so I bought it.

Sanya, at the time, told me that I was a "stupid": "It is not worth more than twenty; the important thing is that you liked her fairy tales."
- If the story is a fairy tale, then this lady is better than me in inciting imaginations. I bought it because it is from Egypt. Do you know what Egypt means to Arabs?
Sanya laughed: The first failed coup.
- No, my dear, it is the first hope; if Egypt becomes fine, everyone will be. She is not the mother of the world; she is the mother of hope.
- We see Syria like this and Iraq too. All siblings share the same misery and hope.
-Sanya. I know what is happening economically, high prices, some arrogant officials, and the presence of thieves of the poor's bread is a handful. However, this is about to disappear; we saw the hope of the Egyptian youth during the days of the revolution.
Egyptians were and still reject idols.
- No, Alia, the situation is worse than you expect; the people are divided into three groups: There is an oath with the current regime, another oath with the Muslims Brotherhood party, and a party with the old government. One party against everyone and another with everyone.
- You mean five groups?
- No three, because I do not believe in the sectarianism of the last two sections; in the last two sections, there is a small hope that the story of the candy jug is accurate, and I do not want to kill this hope.
I don't care if she is an opposition or a loyalist; I want her to be a friend!
I walked in Cairo and Sanya. She was like Egypt, in my opinion: Gorgeous, strong, determined. She was full of ambition and determination.
Her black braided hair told me the story of the three hues, while her childish arrogance only wanted to tell me about hope.
In Egypt, food has a story, the air has a story, drinking has a story, and sex has a story. In the country of mysterious pyramids, novels are born every second.
This is how the jug of candy sat in my American apartment, reminding me every day of my trip to Egypt, reassuring me about Ali and that love works miracles.

Today I saw five tiny houses. I didn't like any of them.

I have a lot of requirements for the new house; I want it to be home!
Therefore, it should be sunny, with a high ceiling and a large kitchen, because cooking is a hobby that only those who pioneered believing stories of reality can master. Sharing food with loved ones is a human art.

I want big windows because hope loves the sun.

I often see homes on the market for sale are ruled by inconsistent glamor and devoid of taste.

The real estate broker who helps me is a lazy man who can only say:
-Its price is reasonable, and I think your demands are challenging to meet.

Umniah showed me an app on the phone to search for homes. It gives you all the information you need about the house. That's how my search became more accessible.

Especially since I can filter search by the number of rooms, price, and other properties.

The large windows were not among the specifications that could be filtered through it, so the pictures were of great benefit too.
****

My sadness mediated my days like a necklace hanging from the long neck of an Arab woman with beautiful Kurdish eyes.

Life has had a heavier and deeper meaning. This is the definition of "logic depression."

Forget about medicine, Alia. Forget about psychiatrists who claim to know the secrets of the soul and the mind!

The more we know life, the more logical depression becomes a reality.

I read the Syrian letters every day and the scraps of paper scattered around my apartment.

The issue of buying a new house cannot get me out of the cycle of the curse.

The whirlpool of being born in beautiful spots of this world. However, our stubborn governments made our homelands nests of migration.

We left the places, but the memories refused to leave us; we carry them on our backs, explain their roots, analyze their developmental history, and wish we could see them!

We try to look at the back and see nothing. We look like fools!

People are walking with their heads held high and looking forward, and we are looking for the source of this weight on the back.

What is more painful than carrying an unseen back bag?

****

Syria is not what it used to be.

I cried alone in that narrow corner; no one saw me as "no one sees weak people."

I cried all my disappointments, from my childhood, in which I only remember the narrowness of my shoes, to adolescence, which did not change anything of my narrow place.

I cried about all the religions I embraced, and those I felt were too big for me.

I cried for all the neighbors' girls and the mouses who gnawed the handles of my empty cupboards' drawers and filled the imagination with "cheese"!

I cried lawless homelands under the name of religion or the title of sultans.

I was crying a little, then turned around a little. No one was looking, so I continued to be comforted until my mother's voice reached me:

"Men do not cry shyly, Ali. Instead, they explain the blessing of tears.".

After that, I cried out loud and got some rest.

When I got that email, I cried too.

Yasmine, the Syrian girl he cut across the oceans to adopt -as well as his homeland- left and did not return.

And other details.

5- We Have God

If you want to forget sadness, failure, disappointment, or even a person, you must turn it into an idea!

I spend this beautiful morning with my lovely Saudi friend "Umniah" and the charming Sudanese "Nile."

Nothing makes me happier than seeing intelligent and polite women; they are all mothers - even without children- who give birth to ambition and hope.

-Homemakers change sponges every month, while they forget to change love sponges.

-What do you mean?

-When love rules the relationship, it comes with a cleaning sponge!

Love works like a sponge, absorbing a person's mistakes, life's difficulties, boredom, and problems.

This sponge needs constant renewal; otherwise, misfortunes begin.

 Love ends when our ability to compromise and absorb problems ends.

Reading books, continuing to learn, and building new friendships and new hobbies all give you a new sponge.

Even silly formalities matter:

Changing the clothing style - while continuing its simplicity - changing the haircut and other material changes suit the owner's individuality.

Relationships ruled by boredom end with the end of the torrent, while the sponge's relationships remain as the springs of fresh water.

-God bless you, Alia! Who hears will say you are the lady in the love's kingdom, start the fortune and get married.

-I'm waiting for you to do it first, Nile, so I'm encouraged.

-Introduce me to Gaim, and I'll do it.

-You got it.

-The woman is the one who makes the man, her ability to make any dream in him stops when she stops loving him.
Umniah smiled and said:
-The most important thing about marriage is choosing the right husband; otherwise, you will spend your life crying over your murdered dreams while having the killer in your bed.
Speaking of the distorted versions, how is the Syrian opposition. I heard that they are effective only in talking.
- Unfortunately, most of them have loud voices and evil thoughts.
On that day, I wrote on Facebook:
When I pass on the Syrian opposition's speeches occupying fancy hotels, hope holds me for a moment; however, after I read their assessments and plans، I lose it.
With all my medical degrees, psychoanalysis training, and philosophy that I got, with all the books I've read and the ones I've imagined, despite all the metaphors of the Arabic language, allegories, and symbols. And with all the polite cursing words in the dictionaries of the wise.
I don't use " so what!" nor " to hell."
The fit expression is "screw this "fancy" opposition."
Imagine who responded to this post with:
-"Thank God you're not here; otherwise, you will make sure you didn't misinterpret. And they deserve it.".
The Syrian
Ali replied, then sent another long message, maybe compensation for all the crazy moments I swore he was alive.
I read and repeated it, then copied it and distributed copies in the corners of the house.
****

Ammar lived in Baghdad until it became part of his heart. He almost forgot Abeer, perhaps completely. She is in Lebanon, "far from the eye, far from the heart."
Heba deservedly filled his free time until she filled the void in his heart.

She volunteered to work with the United Nations, so he joined her and helped in clinics, hospitals, and the Civil Registry Office, he followed her. She wrote against the regime, so he became an opponent.

He analyzed the personalities around her and gave her free advice. While she, like the imaginary queens of Babylon, follows her brain and heart and does not accept a male's control.

The letter on Heba's door was neither a threat nor a love letter; it was the bill for the grocer's account with a note: "We don't accept women with no Hijab in the shop anymore."

She did not know whether she needed to cry or laugh. Iraq in a holocaust, offering sacrifices of world trade, the Silk and Oil Roads got occupied while some males' brains moved to in between thighs!

The next day, this story was part of her lecture on the necessity of revolution in Iraq.

Heba said that the extremist solution would bring more calamities to our grandchildren's future. Instead, she called for embracing the spirit of Tunisia in the land of Mesopotamia.

After the end of the lecture, several extremists followed her. Some of them insulted her; another group told her she didn't deserve to belong to the Holy sect of Shia.

- We are at war. Our enemy is Israel only. Do you want us to sell our land? Do you like us to display our girls without coverage for sale?

The speaker introduced himself as a surgeon and said he graduated from the Sharia Faculty in Egypt.

Heba replied:

-Do you see me as a "sex slave"? If this is the case, review your faith in God who created me!

Then she directed her question to her friend Nigma:

- What did you do in Tunisia so that all the people are under one liberal flag?

Nigma, the beautiful girl of Tunisia, sighed. She looked at the male standing before her, foaming and frothing. She saw his unkempt beard agreeing with his tongue and saw the poison in his eyes - snakes live in the eyes too -. She stood tall, as green as Tunisia.

-"We can't do anything...we are at war!"

At the very least, change the mandatory religious education in public schools to teach morals and empathy from all the prophets and messengers.

Teach children about the saints, the righteous, the advocates of peace, and human rights activists.

It is better than teaching children from the softness of their nails the afflictions of partisanship and testing them in the lies of history!

Turn mosques into homes of morals by stopping some leaders from speaking on God's behalf. Open them to women before men.

Teach children music, singing, poetry, and drawing in them.

Turn them into ideal homes for God instead of being tambourines for the breeding of extremists, not Muslims.

-Are you serious?! Do you want to turn the mosque into a "cabaret"?

-I am sorry for your shallowness! Is teaching children hobbies that help refine their personalities and keep them away from deviation towards terrorism and other things like disco-making?

No, "Doctor," I did not and will not mean that.

The younger generation needs a childhood in which these mosques can contribute free because children are beloved of God, and God is beautiful and loves beauty. We are spirits from God on earth, and we must respect them.

Here, Heba interrupted the conversation, looked at the bearded young man with poisoned eyes, and said:

- Let me wake you up; It did not happen that clubbers blew themselves up in a school bus; they did not spread sermons calling for hatred of a particular religion or sect. They did not make the reputation of religion a fear, and the importance they didn't participate in the worldwide islamophobia.

 Your bearded idols proclaimed a fake history and poisoned a promised future with their paradise for sex; the most sordid "cabaret" known to humankind is what they promised naive after encouraging them to kill the innocents.

 God is not a terrorist, and I do not expect God to blow himself up in innocents in any tale or legend.

Here Ammar entered and pulled Heba and Nigma from the place.

-They stabbed our back; those pretending to care about Palestinian rights. In this life, we owe allegiance to those who stabbed our back; without them, the stab would have been in the middle of the heart, don't be sad!

By the way, imagine this puritan "Doctor" recently did get American citizenship.

He is here for a short visit. Imagine that after he specialized in America and lived from its goodness, he is not grateful to its land, nor did he learn to be a human supporter.

He is still on his maladaptive commitment and own illusions.

Whenever I see people like him inhabiting America, while embassies refuse to grant us the right to visit our families, I know how Trump succeeded in the elections. Those in charge of immigration and human rights affairs there need lessons in the Eastern Mediterranean culture and to recognize the difference between Islam, sects, and extremism.

Ammar put the two girls at Heba's place and bid them farewell:

- If there is any threat to either of you, tell me, I met a group of honest and faithful young men, and they will stand with us.

-Nigma, could you please get into the house? I want to talk to this brave man. Heba said.

Ammar smiled, and genuine happiness flashed in his eyes.

As they paved the streets of Baghdad with the impressions of their feet, Heba told him many tales. Her stories for him were more beautiful than the tales of Scheherazade.

She told him about a journalist who tried to persuade her to sing instead of the press work.

And about a woman who tried to insult her: "Just a rebellious girl."

She told him about her visit to the community clinic when a pregnant patient broke her heart with many questions:

-What should I do so my son will look like my husband?

Ammar laughed:

 - Why would he look like someone else?

- No. The patient's cousin was killed by her husband after giving birth to a blond, white child with colored eyes, while all families are from the oldest grandfather owns a dark brown color.

The truth emerged later: the child had a medical problem called "angel child" syndrome. However, as no one cares about him, he is the "son of the Haram." Yet the baby followed his mother to where there was an honor, not "claiming and pretending."

The naive patient was afraid of fate and predestination because the spokesmen of God interfered even in decree and destiny.

- And they ask, why don't our dreams resemble us in the homelands?!

-Either they are not your dreams but rather the dreams of those you follow without thinking, or there is a syndrome of ignorant time that does its work and kills all the angels' plans.

- Iraq to a revolution, Heba.

Heba smiled, then put her hand on Ammar's cheek:

-I hope.

He took her back to her tiny room, waved goodbye, and felt that her touch remained with him and that his cheek was still smiling.

Ammar touched it in turn and smiled.

****

Abeer left the last cultural gathering that raised the problem of the Syrians in Lebanon crying as usual. Diyar followed her. He tried to speak, and she indicated to him to shut up.

- Better to have your enemy inside the tent pissing out than outside the tent pissing in." *

Then he kept silent.

She walked with him in the beautiful streets of Beirut.

After a distance that looked like bread and butter of silence, Abeer said:

-I believe them only on one condition; they go to their countries and join what they call a revolution of freedom and dignity. Is it reasonable for them to flee from the honor of the resistance?

They did not leave anyone away from their evil. The country has turned into "Afga-Somal," and they are still discussing the best and the future! Fools, they blame the tyrannical regimes for gagging their mouths, then defame every opinion that contradicts their arrogance.

They only care about settling old scores and covering up the grudges that eat them while the homeland is in ruins.

They are trying to legislate many laws; they all have nothing to do with justice or coexistence. They want revenge and don't care if innocent people pay all the taxes. The legislator is the West, and the price is Syria's promised oil to some first-world countries.

-Do you think that any Arab regime will allow a voice of disagreement to have an echo?

It is expected when a dictatorship prevents opinionated brains from participating in their homeland's future and cuts their tongues.

Tongues sprout again! But they grow without connection with their brains.

The regimes that know their only savior is ISIS will never be an option.

He repeated an American politician's statement in English this time.

Abeer smiled:

- This is a summary of what political professionals do in America!

- What would have happened if these people had spoken from inside Syria. What would have happened if the thieves in the government had not eaten the poor's right to freedom of thought, a job, four walls, and a grave?

- I know that what you are saying is logical. I was not surprised by what happened in the country. Most young people searched for immigration for a long time before the war.

I was astonished by the hatred of acculturation. Haven't you heard that hatred swallows up countries?!

They were blinded by hatred and then caught between two fires:

The fire of acknowledging their mistake and embracing half of the truth only.

 - What was the other fire?

-The other is their herd fire. If they stood against it, they would be killed. Their conquests continue, and our calamities carry on.

- I remembered that you were in opposition to the old regime, and I learned that you are in opposition to the new administration, whether it was a fresh one, an envoy, or a renewed one.

- We have God, my comrade. We have God.

6- Dear Scheherazade Please Cook!

Darling,
You are nothing but my baby's fingers
Color
Define the contours of a frame
For a painting
I bought it for my ambition
I said
Will renew the place!
I will change lives with a novel image
I put it all in the corner of my heart
It exhausted the place
I moved it
I placed it leaning on the window of the soul
The wind flew it away
I moved it
I put it wrapped in my mind's library
It dusted
The dust has a memory above the memory
Memories hurt me
So, I moved it
I put it in the kitchen
In the bathroom
And over my morning coffee
It got wet!
It wasn't a gentle way to treat paintings
I spread it on the clothesline
 let it dry
Neighbors grumble
They ruined my reputation

for seduction!
I moved her
folded her
Told her
Put yourself in my pocket
She rebelled
She ran away
Time scattered
I don't know the date of yesterday
My homeland... My love
See
I forgot that parting tears the place
Stop the clocks
And steal paintings.

On a beautiful sunny day, I entered a small house for sale; it had no high ceiling nor big windows.
 Its walls were not white, and its kitchen was not extensive.
I mean, it was far away from what I wanted, but I had strange security and peaceful feelings in it. Then, in the backyard, a hummingbird flew around me; hummingbird is my favorite thing in nature.
And a magic sense spread:
 This is your home, and only you will be the resident.
The house needs a lot of work: Painting, new kitchen, flooring.
The garden looks completely neglected too.
I offered what I could pay - much lower than the listing price -.
I had a prophecy that this house would be my home.
I believe some souls inhabit places and welcome you as the place's owner from the moment you enter; more than this, they hinder the purchase of the house by others.
The real estate agent told me:
- I don't think they will accept this price; raise it a little.
I replied:
- Please try if they don't accept; I don't want the house.

I told Nile what had happened, then invited her to dinner with me and the distinguished dentist, Gaim.

It was the first meeting for the Moroccan with the Sudanese; they were gorgeous together!

The house in my mind was my home, and that day, I got the Syrian message after a long break.

The message from "Ali" was long and drifting in love and humanity. I have read it fifty-five times so far!

My scleroderma was too weak to deprive me of the pleasure of imagination. So I went - hypothetically - with Ali to Iraq and Syria.

I read the following passage more than once; another prophecy bloomed in my heart that the magical solution to the war lies between these lines:

"I lived in Syria in areas belonging to the Kurds. I got acquainted with the honest man Castro; a doctor took a loaf of Tannour bread* in exchange for an examination to help the poor, and if the patient was hungry, he gave him the loaf of the previous patient.

This Castro taught me to love the earth and its people, so I'll gain the love of the sky.

That is why Castro dreamed of a homeland for the Kurds.

He told me that Arab nationalism had never recognized him as Kurdish; it didn't accept him as equal to others or respected him belonging first to Kurdistan.

What else to tell you about Castro?

He has a Yazidi girlfriend, Nineveh. He will marry her soon.

She was a captive of the savages. Yes, the caliphate state ،ISIS and whoever is wrapped around it.

She told us in a voice choked by tears about what happened in Sinjar and the great day of the massacre. She said:

-*"They attacked us like hungry wild ghouls. It is enough for anyone to see or hear of them to make Islam apostasy, with no prayer after it. They killed hundreds.*

*They took women and children as spoils of war. I became a Milk Al-Yameen. ***

My religion was Yazidis. To simplify it, I say to you:

We gather goodness from all religions. Our religion is a union of Zoroastrianism, Islam, Christianity, and Judaism.

They told me I must become a Muslim, and unfortunately, "Islam" is, in their view: The niqab and the saying of the two testimonies.

What else do I tell you?

I got to know Tamadour. They say she is ugly - and I don't see any woman ugly-they almost killed her. So, I convinced the "prince" to keep her life because she cooked well. And I managed to save my life because I am good at making sweets.

Tamadour was better than Scheherazade in spreading her delicious cooking amulets.

How did I bear what I endured?

The spirit of Lady Zaynab* left her shrine and accompanied me until I entered Syria. This is what I convinced myself of:

The ISIS raid of the Yazidis coincided with their bombing of the shrine of Sayyida Zainab* in Sinjar. And the killing of those who guarded it.

Then I saw white Zaynab* flowers in my sleep, and I woke up with a feeling of an aura that resides in my forehead, an atmosphere that resembles her soul. She protected me and cured my soul.

Zaynab, the daughter of Fatima al-Zahra and Imam Ali, and Prophet Muhammad's granddaughter. Zaynab, who was taken captive one day like me. She was not defeated and did not allow the immoral people to win.

That is why I am here, and I will marry Castro, the man who deserves Zaynab's likenesses. This great man protects the display of all religions.".

Nineveh and Castro were examples of a safe house and a bright future. What else can I tell you, Alia, the Highest*?

Only a tiny piece of my heart remained to pump blood into the memory, so the memories became my diary and future. This was what psychiatry calls "post-traumatic stress syndrome" or PTSD, isn't it, wise doctor?

The Iraqi and then the Syrian war cut off all my arteries to dreams.

I watched my dreams die with the dear ones I lost, who returned to the sky. People who stayed on earth had changed by their will or against it.

Life on this part of the earth is like hell, but it is without windows.

You will tell me: It has doors.

And I will answer: There are many doors, but thieves and bandits, as prisoners of poverty, do not have the keys.

You will say: I am not one of them.

I will answer: How do you move freely in a place full of whom you want to escape from and whom you want to help?

The Kurds and the Yezidis are not like the Arabs. They look like the chivalrous Arabs. I am sure that you will ask why I put them together. Many say the Yezidis are a religion and the Kurds are a nation.

I put them together simply because it is between the two groups: Many Arab kings' honor is lost.

What happened to the Kurds and the Yazidis under Arab governments. The marginalization and the attempts to imprint were unfair.

It was like what happened to the Jewish under some Arabs in the past. That is why I sympathized with these groups and implicitly belonged to them.

As for Syria, y'* Syrian:

Dr. Muhammad, listen; people here are not the same. No house didn't have a cup or two of death.

No wall didn't hang a picture with a black ribbon in its heart.

People's eyes hide the whole story; you see oppression and poverty in their sadness and angry tone of voice.

I don't see stability soon or any victory even far away.

****

On a beautiful night in Baghdad, the sky filled with saints. Each of them sat on a star and accepted supplications.

Ammar was praying to God to get the heart of Heba. He knew that her mind was very private property.

He said to his friend once:

- I do not know how to describe my feelings toward her. As Emil Cioran said: "Forty-thousand years of human language, and you cannot find a single word that completely describes the feeling inside you."

Heba was popular in getting girls together as she brought them closer with common jealousy from her. This means that the girls become friends because of their mutual jealousy of Heba.

Jealousy is a parasitic feeling that needs others' alive ambition to survive!

In her last article, Heba spoke about cosmetics and the ability of some women to appear as another person.

She said: Turning women into paintings is like covering them with the niqab.

She also said: This miserable ignorance phase of sex and radicalism has replaced the time of love, and unfortunately, the woman has become a vulva and lips to some people. Some women excel in showing them for the sake of the male, or some males master covering them for the "penis."

The demand to stop covering women is a legitimate right during the time of Sexual jihad*. It is the first step to escape from ISIS and harassment in the defeated Arab countries!

However, this time, Heba's article did not pass peacefully.

The pretenders of Islam brought it to the Islamists, who transformed it, then brought it to the religious authorities after it became distorted and hostile against Islam.

7- Go On; God Is With You

My Jewish grandmother had told me about Iraq a hundred years ago.
She said the head covering was strange in the cities and for protection from the sun in the villages.
I was little, skinny but "chubby with questions," how not, and my grandmother's time seemed like a fairy tale!
She told me about chivalry, pardon, forgiveness, the purity of the souls and early sleep habits, the croaking of frogs in the stillness of the nights, and the sound of birds with the flute of tandoor bread clay ovens in the villages.
Grandma told me about friends' debates and maneuvers of lovers.
She also said that people were more straightforward:
-They were communicating with their eyes, not their phones. She told me about the borders and how they drew them cleverly.
- We used to call that whole region Al-Sham. Its name was derived from Sam the Prophet, the son of Noah. So that is why I told you to name your child Sam.
- How old are you, grandma?
-From the age of the borders.
-Are you Muslim?
-No, I am Jewish, but I would not have been able to marry your grandfather if I had not pronounced the two testimonies.
Questions revolve in my little head:
-What does this have to do with that?
****

-I learned that life is playing with us. She is a child who does not grow up ‹while we are aging and getting old.

Our details that don't get old are our meaningful minutes, novel thoughts, attitudes, deep sadness, joyful details, the looks in our eyes, and memories of our successes and failures.

However, our pictures, hairstyle, clothes, in brief, our outside scales change a lot.

With all the above, you make a clear picture of yourself!

These are what draw our image in others' eyes. But our whole picture judges others, not us.

-How? Please give me an example.

-Sure. When someone remarked badly on a woman's clothes, he openly declared looking at women with instinct before brain.

He gave an impression about himself, not about the woman.

-Right in the virtual world, our words resembled us.

-I know you through your words, so if you see me once in a public park, would you say to me: Thanks for what you write, or read my writings through another mind!

-Virtual space has its bridges with reality.

I wrote this during a virtual conversation with Sanya, and a small note came to me; the realtor sent a message.

-The sellers accepted another offer, more money than we put down; sorry, we will look for a new house.

-Thank you, it's not a problem.

And I said to myself:

I was wrong. Maybe I should have raised the price. I followed my sixth sense more than I was supposed to.

****

The following day, I woke up fresh as usual; nothing in life is better than eight hours of continuous night sleep.

Nile came for morning coffee and entered the apartment with her energy halo as usual:

-What happened with the house?

I smiled:

- My sixth sense is no longer working, the house is gone, so I don't trust it anymore.

-I will continue to trust it; my relationship with Gaim is the best evidence.

- I'm happy about this, but I lost the house.

-Did they sell it?

- They will. They accepted another offer.

-The house will come back to you, you'll see.

-Now you believe in magic, Nile?

-A good, faithful friend inspired by God. Don't worry!

-Thank you!

-Please read my coffee cup*.

- To tell you about what?

-About the simplest things like my ability to get the beautiful young man Gaim, also tell me about the most complex, like the future of our Arab countries.

- As for Gaim, you can get him in the blink if you want. The secret of the recipe is to neglect him.

As for your complicated question:

 How can I open a cup and read about the future of strangeness at the bottom?

Turn on the TV and watch the farce with your own eyes, or, my dear, read in the virtual space.

We believe our cups more than the newspapers of countries we fled from. Does that mean anything to you?

- I want you to use your sixth solid sense. We in the black culture associate with coffee and love it.

Beautiful coffee suggests equality, the equality I lost in Arab countries and the West of "freedom."

Racism is eating me, Alia, and with my Hijab, the mud has become muddy.

Even Gaim. I think he does not like to marry a black girl.

-If this is the case, he does not deserve you.

Nile, you know that love knows no shape or color. It is the first unifier of people.

The sexual attraction is subject to form, and not all love is sexᶜ; otherwise, it would have nothing of magic.

Whoever wants to put you down -for whatever reason- will find something that separates you from him, even if you look exactly like him.

- Their racism in Arab countries was against my color; here, their racism was against my color and religion.

I know that you took off your Hijab one day, and racism was one of your reasons. But I got used to my Hijab. Although I consider it a habit, not an obligation, and I do not believe in its position as evidence of faith or fidelity, it is my right to dress as I want.

-I removed the veil because I will not continue a habit that turns day after day into a wrong title of honor.

Racism in Arab countries was against my removal of it; many spat on me. Could you believe that some women accepted the humiliation of their sisters for the sake of a cloth that does not indicate morals?

-I know, Dr. M…Nile said with a smile.

-The Hijab is an outfit and a personal choice of clothes with decency. But it will never become a sign of faith.

Then she smiled and continued: For God's sake, read me the cup.

- Ok, Nile, in your cup is a little child sitting on the threshold of your mind; you will not get him unless you open your heart.

Nile laughed:

-His name is Gaim!

****

When Ammar lived in Iraq, it did not occur to him that he was Sunni by birth and lived in Shiite areas.

His honesty was enough not to put a barrier between one sect and another.

Everyone believed he was an Iraqi Shia or Syrian Alawi in the new neighborhood.

 He visits the shrine of Imam Ali* every week:

-Dear Imam Ali, do you not see what happened to us? Do you not see how religion has become mere husks and deceptive appearances?

Where is the work, and where are the workers? How can a country whose oil is more than its water live in the dark?

77

He once said to Heba:

- The situation would have been better if the Sunnis had three eyes and the Shiites had two noses. At least we know how they differ and why they argue?

She laughed while saying:

-I want two tongues; I'll join any religion that gives me the right to have them.

She paused, then continued:

We have forgotten the meaning of religion; sects are just an escape to contain our disappointments:

Barefoot children fill the streets; orphans have no place, disfigured from war are ostracized, while we, y'* we:

We raise the flags of women's veils, males' beards, and Zabiba*.

We argue about the priority of one sect or one king's right over another one.

Iraq, Syria, Egypt, Morocco, Algeria, and every spot from the ocean of gas and poverty to the gulf of oil and stifling; the exact epidemic;

Mixing religion with politics, then ruling them over our lives.

Religion was created primarily to defend people and prevent injustice but has turned into a tool of injustice in the hands of politicians and a tool for discrimination between humans. The era of (read) has ended, and a time has begun for: (imitate).

-I understand; I liked your idea in your last article on "reading what you facilitate."

How did it not occur to me before? You are an excellent reader, the idea of books on a mobile phone is fantastic.

It is better than hearing the squawks of some sheiks or the hissing of some "singers" ha!

- Your Tunisian friend, my rival, always takes you from me. How is she?

- She still calls for women's freedom in the societies of "Islam."

Did you know that her father forced her to wear the Hijab at age ten? And when she fled from Tunisia. She ran away from oppression and persecution. They wanted her to get married to an older male.

-It is possible to call yourself a Muslim and at the same time lie, betray, and mention the name of God as an idol in your prayers without thinking about it.

in contrast:

You can be honest, genuine, and gallant, and they call you "infidel" because you believe in humanity and God.

- We are not in a divine court. God is not the public prosecutor, nor they are the judge. Instead, God is merciful and created all human beings with logic.

As some Islamists claim, is it conceivable that most of the world's population will go to hell?

Is it conceivable that women who are Inventors, Writers, Doctors, Teachers, and Mothers are deficient in brains?

-You have a right; God can be a lawyer for each of us.

Religion is how you treat people!

-Exactly, thank you.

-Iraq to a revolution, dear Heba, you'll see.

-I hope for that!

****

Abeer was looking for a new job in Lebanon. In her previous one, the place owner tried to harass her. When she rebelled, he told her:

-You Syrians have eaten each other, and you are arrogant now!

She shouted at him in front of all the people while leaving the place:

- The real Syrians are masters of those with no homeland like you.

You don't deserve the Lebanese nationality, you immoral person.

Lebanon embraces an honorable woman like me.

The way home was long.

Abeer was looking for a new job in Lebanon. In her previous one, the place owner tried to harass her. When she rebelled, he told her:

-You Syrians have eaten each other, and you are arrogant now!

She shouted at him in front of all the people while leaving the place:

- The real Syrians are masters of those with no homeland like you.

You don't deserve the Lebanese nationality, you immoral person.

Lebanon embraces an honorable woman like me.

The way home was long.

Abeer felt that the losses that borders between countries bring are less than those caused by the idea of one nationalism or the only religion.

On the sidewalks, working Syrian children filled the place. Each has a story and a tale with a lump in the heart.

They chant without thinking infected sentences they learned from the political trend they are working under its sick roof.

In Beirut, wealth is colorful, while poverty is enveloped in the death color, regardless of the political trend.

Diyar, who suddenly appeared in her life, works in a bank, even though he is a graduate of Arabic literature: Work crises here haunt even those with Lebanese citizenship.

He started his talk with her that day with a definition of the revolution.

The revolution is the natural development of these countries when nepotism and stratified steal the homeland and trade in the dreams of its youth.

It is the natural development of losing the future of the youth due to corruption and officials' "law."

Shutting down the intellectuals' minds while releasing the arms and tails of the pretenders and beards carry priceless taxes.

The transformation of the revolution into an armed conflict, a civil war, and a stab in the heart of the country is the natural development of corrupt regimes' inability to win over young people's lost minds.

The natural evolution of millions of dollars spent on Sharia colleges and houses of worship while brains flee searching for a homeland!

This was their tenth meeting. Diyar told Abeer that he was trying to travel to Canada, and his friends were trying to travel too.

- What a country whose young men race to leave it! What a country! Unfortunately, I don't think there are many exceptions in the Arab countries.

-What about the oil countries?

-Do you mean Iraq?

-The Gulf Cooperation Council countries.

- I think its residents are trying to leave for other reasons: repression, education, and racism against certain Islam sects.

-You are prejudiced against Arabs, ha! This is not true; Many want to go to work in the United Arab Emirates.

- I am not prejudiced; I am sad; I know that kindness and generosity are common in their nature; however, what is happening makes me sad. Why did we switch from reading books to reading fortune telling? Why did we turn from a title for civilization to a title for terrorism? I am sad and in pain; my great country hurts me.

-Why are you not looking for a job in Iraq?

-Are you serious?

-Yes, many of my friends work there with excellent salaries.

-I'll try; now, let me go back to my idea and clarify it.

The regimes remain the first - not the only - responsible for losing homelands.

Whoever says other than this is afraid, a coward, or wants to silence the voice of his conscience so his eyes may sleep well.

May God bless our good people in countries we have left, but they still live in us.

Abeer smiled:

-I'm a coward!

- I didn't mean you, but I'm sad. Do you expect the situation in Lebanon to get better soon? No. It will explode quickly, as in every Arab country. Governments no longer have room for hypocrisy, twisting, and revolving in this virtual time.

This is the time of all cultures cooked in one pot. Do you know what it means to cook the " equality" Western fish with expired sour Arabic milk? The result is indigestion.

-Why don't Westerners eat?

-They have the right to cook on their own, and they guarantee the dignity of sitting around food and the right to be full.

-I told you I'm a coward.

Diyar approached one step, then two steps. Then, he embraced Abeer with all his arms in a magical moment.

-You are not a coward. You are alone.

He was silent for a while and added:

-Alone like me, just like me.

****

I tricked this life with a slender waist, brown skin, and black eyes.
I told the misfortunes, come alone and do not gather on my back!
A hump does not look good above my chest or my shoulders.
I did not know that a woman's femininity is not complete without her strength, defying difficulties, and her right not to be subordinate to males so she keeps up with real men.
Iraq has always been here in the heart of memory. Walking barefoot on safe childhood whispers to me:
-A woman who drank from Iraqi water is the queen of all women.
She doesn't accept being broken or defeated and won't give up on failure but would make it a success.
The women of Iraq broke the collar of the Hareem* and taught the world how women are.
She said:
The premise of the veil is similar to traditional marriage. In many cases, this marriage succeeds, but its failure cases slap religion and humanity.
 What would have happened if a woman's Hijab had turned into a traditional dress like a man's cloak? Whoever wants to wear it, let her do it of free will.
The Qur'an is a book of metaphors, and the verses that some say encourage the veil are only metaphors for the necessity of mental concealment and self-respect. Just like the verse of cutting off the hand of a thief, for example.
Cutting off the hand of the thief means to prevent him from stealing. Therefore, it is unreasonable for God to want his servants mutilated and unemployed as a punishment.
The harshest punishment is fixing the defect and blocking the way to repeat it.
Some veiled women are real and strong; I see them, but it is not our case. I do not understand how some veiled women accept the veil's transformation into an obligation!
Yet, they suppress many women who reject " the covering" idea and indirectly force them to wear hijabs in many societies.

I am not against the freedom to choose to clothe, but I am against imposing a particular dress on women and considering women as flawed beings; they need someone to decide on their behalf, while males possess power and influence, and nothing but ruin reaches our nations. I fled from Tunisia from the oppression of my family; from women's oppression, forcing me to wear Hijab was a prelude to forcing me to marry. Listen to what happened.

They shed my blood, and my brother followed me to Egypt. He tried to kill me. Can you imagine? He used my mom as bait.

He told me:

- Your mother is sick. She wants to see you.

- My mother called me - via Facebook - an hour before meeting him and told me that he was lying and that he was crazy and wanted to kill me "to protect his honor."

Imagine Heba; My mother resorted to a strange girl in the street to send me the message via Facebook that she heard from her neighbors.

She told me that she did not sleep because I was not well and asked me to flee to another country and not tell anyone about my location. And more than that. To change my name, can you imagine?

She said to me: Forget your old name and delete this page. You will be a star in the sky of my soul, and I will meet you in another life or with God! Be well and go now.

That night I went to Jordan, then Iraq. No one would ever think that I would seek refuge in Iraq. Since that night, my name has become Nigma* of the Sabah. Sabah* is my mother's name.

Heba cried with Nigma. Nothing builds strong friendships more than crying together!

Heba knows that her last article opened the eyes of the Sultan's dogs and the religions' merchants. But in the story of Nigma today was a divine message to Heba:

 "Go on, Heba...God is with you ".

8- The Date of Our Death Passes In Front of Us Every Year

It felt like on a different day
A pink day in a blue world
A day when I have the right to dream
How difficult a dream will be if your dictionary does not (bribe) life!
I braided my brown hair, which was not cursed by the colors of the merchants.
And on my face:
I put a smile in the place of lipstick and hope instead of eyeliner!
Perhaps today will be a future date for a party where I will wear a white dress.
A party that does not resemble a noisy drums party:
Friends will take pictures of us on the beach.
Then we'll go to dinner in a simple restaurant that used to serve jasmine to the newlyweds.
Today in today is similar to today in tomorrow. We live our future without knowing.
We live the day of our success, our failure, the birth of the first dream, and the first child. Even the date of our death passes in front of us every year.
I wrote it on my happy day when the second letter of "the absent" arrived.
****

Oh, my Lord, kill the zealots before civilization ends, as it ended in the old days.
I watched the massacres of ISIS against the Syrians, eating hearts, raping children, selling women, and speaking on God's behalf!

Anger and helplessness surrounded my simplicity; the question that baffles me:

Why don't Muslims revolt against ISIS?

Why don't they defend their peace?

How do they demonstrate against high prices, corruption, and regimes while they do not care about cancer spreading in the body of their countries from the ocean to the Gulf?

Whenever I write something on Facebook, many people steal it and adopt it, which means they support the idea, so why not encourage it? Only noble hearts share my publications and books. They know that spreading ideas during the time of the thinking Niqab is a zakat* to support our grandchildren's future.

I was thinking deeply while drinking my coffee on the quiet banks of the American lake.

The beaches here belong to the poor before the rich, and there is no room for their monopoly.

Nile invited me to brunch, a meal between early breakfast and lunch. It can be considered the natural breakfast in eastern countries - where people wake up late on holidays or neglect the benefits of breakfast on regular days and eat late. Or simply poverty prevents some people from eating in the morning -.

Everything here makes me live in both places at the same time!

In my heart lives some sad thoughts and some hopeful ones.

I have a conception that is not devoid of logic that humanity has reached the same time as globalization and missiles in the past; the pharaohs, for example, knew the mobile phone and the personal computer, and they got to the moon. They sank to the bottom of the seas. Just as each of us has many lives, the planet Earth has more lives, but its lifespan is thousands of years in every life.

Perhaps mixing religion with politicians spoiled places in the old days. And this is what will happen again if people do not use their brains. Religions did not come again but were repeated for humans. In every life on this planet, there were divine religions that called for the good of people if they used their minds.

Religions are like revolutions; the beneficiaries ride them!

- The Arab community in the diaspora is not better than others. Backstabbing and gossip are the same in our country.
-The few here seized their knowledge and morals, so they came out independent, not imitating their predecessors with naivety, and did not copy their emigration stupidly!
- The situation in Dubai is not better. Although the place radiates architectural and economic civilization, society still needs the awakening of a book. Or, as Alia says: the awakening of psychiatry!
- Regardless of what you say. I believe that if the UAE government continues to spend oil money on developing the country, this beautiful place will not have a global competitor. But if the extremists take over, the area will go into the path of Iraq; what is the case?
How is your work there?
- Work is different; it is not like it in Lebanon. I work seriously every day for nine hours. I have one day off Friday; I meet patients of all nationalities. I use the English language. I know that I'll reap the result of my hard work at the end of the month, and despite the high prices in Dubai, life is lovely!
Nile smiled and asked:
- You don't have gossip?
And Gardy replied with a laugh:
-That's all over the world.
Gardy is an abbreviation of Gardenia, and Gardenia is a mutual friend of Nile and Umniah. She lived as a neighbor for them in America with her husband and two daughters.
She lived the bitterness of an unsuccessful marriage as well as Umniah, but she was braver than her.
She went to Dubai on a trip and did not return. She divorced her husband on a moonless night. There were many rumors about her divorce, but the ophthalmologist was greater than all the arrogants' words. She embraced her two children and worked hard.
Her husband traveled to another state, and the rumor said that he married a semi-illiterate woman - as he could not try to tame more educated women -.

As for Gardenia, she comes to visit us while attending any conference in America.

Gardy is very grateful to the UAE. She thanks its rulers daily.

With every bombing in the East, Gardy holds her heart in her hand with her two children in it.

Today, she told us about the details of her divorce and how guilt is the deadly killer feeling that cheating husbands try to get rid of when they betray. It causes them to create justifications for neglecting their children for affairs.

This disappointing feeling is negatively reflected on the wives in the form of another stupid but fatal sense of guilt; "I am the reason for my husband's betrayal of insolence."

This makes some wives suffer from obesity or are subject to plastic surgery and blowing.

Instead of protecting their dignity and standing firm and in faith against the husband's injustice, they invited sadness over or started a dramatic new chapter.

I chose to stand my ground and respect myself. When he cheated on me, I left.

On that fine day, I received a realtor's new message:

- The house is back on the market. The owners disagreed with the buyer, who wanted to lower the price to ensure exceptional repairs. Are you still interested in it?

- Very much so, will they accept the price.

- Won't you increase it?

-No, the same price, unfortunately, I can't pay more.

I said, with the image of a hummingbird in my head.

-I'll call them and let you know.

I smiled confidently, not because my sixth sense was still working but because the hummingbird sent me a message, and I believed it!

****

The streets in Iraq are more beautiful than anywhere else because they run to the middle of your heart.

If you are a follower of a poet, words will flow in your blood.

This is the case for the people of knowledge and poetry in Iraq; the words' meaning flows in their blood.

They told him that Heba was in prison, the charge: Contempt for religion.

He cried as he remembered her last singing:

Once upon a time, y' gentlemen, honorable people:

A beautiful religion and some crowns!

The first crown decided to wear the religion, and it was wide

He cut it from the left

The second crown decided to wear the religion, and it was too narrow

It expanded from the right

The third crown chose to wear the religion

He found it short, so he added on "some talks."

And the fourth crown, he found it long

So, he burned some details.

And the fifth

 And the sixth

One hundred, then

One million

A small piece of the religion remained

The politicians competed to trade in it

Marketing its place

While the wise used it as a witness to the necessity of using brains

Once upon a time, y' gentlemen and honorable people

A beautiful religion and some crowns!

To restore religion, we need a revolution against the lies of politicians and the injustice of the crowns.

They told her during the investigation: You incite a revolution, you " uncovered" woman! In your dreams!

They beat and humiliated her.

On the first day, she thought she was strong as long as they were so afraid of her words.

But with sleep deprivation, beatings, and hunger, she began to feel broken and vulnerable.

She remembered the cat she had rescued on a rainy Baghdad night.

She remembered the look of her panic and her helplessness.
She saw in the cat's eyes the mirror of her today!
-God fights them; if all of this does not start a revolution, where is the dignity of the Iraqis?
Heba cuddled her imagination's cat:
- You will live.
She told herself, then fell asleep.

9- The Virtual Space Is The Witness Who Has Not Seen Anything

This restaurant has been for Syrian expatriates since the eighties. First, its name was: "Let your dreams be big." Then its name changed after the Syrian war to "Syria Without Borders."

His reputation is excellent in the state for his cleanliness, the integrity of his companions, and food taste.

I sat and ordered Syrian coffee with cherry; you'll surely do it again when you test them together. Then, I posted this on Facebook:

"Do not believe in your distinction because that will make you think you are above others, and whoever is above people cannot write about them. Egotism will destroy you if you fail, keep you away from the taste of hunger, and turn you into an arrogant monster if you get criticized."

And about 20 minutes, the girls arrived.

-Congratulations on the house!

-Thank you. May God bless your life and dreams!

- Your sixth sense won again, Alia!

-Actually, it was your sixth sense, not mine, and the hummingbird's message.

-Both of you, just feed us now. Umniah laughed and said.

-Thank you all, my sisters, for accepting the invitation; hopefully, next time will be in the house after the repairs and the upgrades.

We ate Shawarma with a Syrian flavor; nothing is better than Syrian Shawarma!

We looked beautiful: Nile in her hijab and bright, colorful clothes. Gardenia in luxurious classic garments; Umniah in the abaya and the lace veil, me in the doctor's blue suit and my braided hair.

Today is Eid; why not dream of a tomorrow in which young people will not leave their countries, beloved ones, and memories?

****

The house I bought looks like havoc. How much time and effort do I need to repair and make my home?

On my journey to find a constructor, I saw many human types. They gave me different numbers.

Every time I told someone I wanted to remove walls to make the kitchen expand, and the border between the living room and the garden would turn into a giant crystal door, the price increased and swung my dream!

Until an honest Lebanese friend told me about José, a Mexican constructor, he showed me pictures of their work at his house.

And he was right!

Jose is competent enough to answer you with the word: "We try" to all your requests.

Then he tries to change them with expert wisdom. I loved his passion for his work and signed a contract with him.

This house will be my little homeland; I will try as much as possible to make it look like me with its simplicity and ability to give souls the comfort to disclose secrets and put down burdens.

****

Sadness still haunts me like a summer cloud; it does not rain and does not accept to cover the sun.

The voices of those who left prevented me from speaking; in my memory, a sad tone of loved ones who went and closed doors to the darkness behind them.

What burns the heart is not them but those who stayed in the place with their bodies only. They became other people, ghosts of those we knew.

Is this what happens when the sky is pleased with you and fulfills your supplication that God preserves them?

They preserve them with other copies, which gratify memory, copies that do not resemble us and do not resemble them".

Heba's crying on the paper had a sad sound. It was like October rain on the hair of a child without parents. She does not sell matches but wipes shoes.

She does not know the cold because it is a luxury. However, she knows a kick she received from a male in the fifties. He decided that he would not pay a child who had no protectors.

After her release from prison, Heba became that child. She didn't have the right to dream, even in a small stable room.

Every day, before she sleeps, she hears the sound of the jailer's footsteps and the sound of strange laughter that does not resemble the kind Iraqi voices.

And although they said they were Iraqis, she was sure that the poisons of Iraq had given birth to them.

Depression enveloped Heba's life, and she became another person. Ammar tried to contact her a lot, but she did not respond. She is ashamed of her failure in front of him and what she said to him. She, too, has joined the generation of defeat.

She read children's stories, in particular, everything written by the Danish creative Hans Christian Andersen:

She read: The Match Girl, The Snow Queen, The Ugly Duckling, The Little Mermaid, and The Emperor's New Clothes.

Those books had an impact that patted her shoulder with hope.

****

At the same time and in a different place, Abeer got lost in the streets of Lebanon.

She did not know how her feet would lead her to a narrow alley with a small shop selling falafel. She felt herself in Syria and smiled more when the seller was Syrian: She said to him:

- Do not ask me where you are from in Syria, or I will not buy*. Then she smiled.

-May God protects you from wherever you are, my daughter.

She burst into tears before answering:

-May God strengthens your vulnerability*

-She went on her way, feeling that her vulnerability strengthened, and the seller's words helped her and lit her way, she would be able to reach her date with Diyar.

The reparation of the Syrians and the Arabs is a heart prayer because we all have a deep wound.

We are wounded by wishes hanging on the windows of our mothers, the memories we left behind, and our dreams.

We got the wound when we chose between staying in the mother's lap or catching up with the dreams.

And when this wound healed, we searched in the hearts of others for another family and sweeter memories.

The whole region is wounded from the ocean to the Gulf, while the beards used that to spread religious extremism.

After the wars and the escalation of poverty and humiliation, many of the wounded hearts felt more helpless, and they had nothing left but religion to resort to.

-Because of human weakness, they wanted to feel their strength and the value of their existence, so they turned to extremists in defense of religion. Thus, religion became a fetish that cannot be debated with reason.

Diyar told her:

 - You expect the situation to calm down, and I tell you, look at Iraq.

By the way, I asked about a job there, and it is possible.

Many educated brains have left Iraq, and there is a need for new cadres. Imagine, just imagine that the Arab countries are innovating in (smuggling) their brains, then they suffer from a shortage of cadres!

And she gave him a portion of the falafel roll:

- I'll go with you, then! May God strengthens your vulnerability*.

****

His letters cross oceans, challenging the non-diplomatic relations between Uncle Sam's country and Syria, The Jasmine*.

How can I sleep while he lives in a border city between the Ibn Taymiyyah Brigade and ISIS bullets?

How did it occur to him to live there? What does this emotional person want? A bullet in the heart won't kill him; it will kill me.

He was not lucky to meet Jasmine, who ended as an oblation made by the world's silence to ISIS.

But he was able to adopt two other children:
Omar, a four-year-old boy, and a six-year-old girl named Raqqa, after the Syrian city of Raqqa, sadly fell under the hands and shoes of ISIS. The parents of the two children were killed, and they were among hundreds of orphans left behind by the toxic war.
They called Ali, daddy on the second day of their meeting.
He wrote to me that he had become a father before he thought about the size of the responsibility awaiting him.
Then he told me that he was trying to travel to his mother's family in Iraq because northern Syria was under the line of fire.
He wrote he is optimistic about the future of Iraq and that he supports me in my belief that Iraq is the father of all Arab countries, and that Egypt is their mother.
If these two countries become well, then everyone will be well.
While I was thinking, his message appeared on the chat window:
Morning evening! As you have the time night, and we have a day now! Is there a philosophical metaphor for this?
-Metonyms evening then! Where have you been for five days?
-I was protesting.
- Are you kidding?
- No, for real!
-Tell me what happened.
- A demonstration went out against ISIS, and I went out with it. Then the extremists came and broke it up.
After that, everyone started chanting against Israel until one decided to chant against the regime. Then, believe it or not, the people were divided between loyalists and opponents of Israel!
You cannot imagine What happened even if you were the most intelligent writer on this earth.
-What's so strange about that? It is expected.
- This is not true. Perhaps you were one of the few who was not surprised by the Syrian / Syrian conflict over the idea of Israel.
Perhaps if the Israeli flag had been raised on this land, all this war would not have happened. I don't know.
-I didn't mean that; I meant no one is surprised.

The majority of people are between parties: the first party: the Loyal to the regimen, the second one supports the opposition, and a third party supports ISIS.

Although the first two parties didn't want ISIS to exist in any way, they indirectly participated in giving it the power and the land!

I was not surprised because I am not an extremist. I see the whole picture and not what I cut off from it. I am from the forgotten fourth party, the neutral party: We don't support anyone, we wanted real revolution, but unfortunately, it didn't work!

-I would never sell our rights; Palestine is our land even after a hundred years; the issues today are different. I know that you care more about peace, and our different opinions would not stand totally apart; we both support humanity.

In general, you are right; may God protect this miserable Middle East.

The hatred in Syria occupies the land and the sky.

The dust of the earth contains hopes, but the soil has the martyred bodies, hidden truths, innocent childhoods, dreamy youths, pure wishes, crushed goals, repressed ideas, and rejected opinions.

Such land will not accept peace or reconciliation.

I must go to Iraq; I have good old friends in Baghdad.

The last time I spoke to someone was four years ago, but I don't think they would oppose my help.

-Why don't you turn to your relatives in Syria?

- All left.

-What do you mean?

- Some of them are in the army for the obligated service.

Some people expatriate to many countries around the world. Some were martyred, and a section in the sky's residence.

-What about your sisters?

- Hoda is still in Germany; she doesn't talk to me.

Hayat and Magda are in Kuwait, and I don't think of living there, at least now.

After that, the communication with Ali was cut off; perhaps the internet networks were terrible because of the war.

I will not think about terrible possibilities.

They say: A person worries all his life about what will not happen so that other calamities will happen to him because of anxiety.

I wrote before I fell asleep:

He is right; such land will not accept peace or reconciliation, and the sky that is crowded with the shattered dreams of youth will not see the supplication.

I look daily at my country ravaged by the cancer of hate with the notorious pancreatic cancer.

I ask myself: Why do we have the right to abandon our homelands before cancer and return to them afterward?

I did not know that the cancer of the homelands is transmitted to us with feelings. Yes, emotions transmit dangerous diseases.

Yes, the Syrian/Syrian conflict does not tolerate theories of right and wrong, halal and haram*. It is the struggle of cancer with a bad prognosis, and it's mortal doomed with hatred.

He is correct; we need the wise, not the extremists; who knows, the issue is no longer the issue of Palestine or Israel alone.

The issue today is not limited to the countries of the Middle East theater. Instead, it extends and extends over the globe's length and diameter, and even if this case uses my dreams and yours as a soundtrack, we have nothing but echoes in it.

It is swarming with directors and authors from the western economic crises and the Gulf of oil and gas.

Today, the wise, those who know that religious fanaticism and military oppression are the enemies of peace. There is no return to any place in the East without allowing the voice of the secular to rise.

Secularists: Those who separate religion from the law. Those who demand the right of expression before the right to self-determination are our hope.

How can we claim any right while silencing the sound of the pen that does not apply kiss ass?

How does any society develop without rational opposition?

How does the country develop while part of the youth is jobless between cafes and Friday extremism sermons? And another part between prisons and exile because of an opinion?

What do we want from tomorrow? Bragging that we're not selling the land? Or solve the issues that eat into the flesh of our children?

The wise only, not the extremists; the brilliant gray shades of truth holders are our hope and will herald a cure; as for the others, they are transient!

To the pens holders of all kinds:

You have to choose between a scream of a bereaved mother or a peaceful childhood for your grandchildren.

Between praising kings or standing in the line of those whom corruption - before the war - ate their dreams.

Between ringing the necks' bells of cheap flocks, opposition selling your homeland, or liberating the feet of youth from the shackles of religious fanaticism.

There is no solution to accepting strictness; the answer is not urging people to leave their religion.

You must choose:

Either you declare it a war against the simple and the poor, against those who believe in religion to save them, or you can use your brains and help them use theirs. Stand by prayers of orphans.

Today's war: A war of ideas and the virtual space is the witness who did not see anything.

10- From God's Place!

When the war approached me for the first time, the situation was dire. I felt myself on a ship in the middle of a raging ocean full of dead bodies. It chased me and asked me for a reason:
-Why did you stay here while the shark ate my hand?
-How did you wave to this life while my child went out and did not return?
-What did you sacrifice? I gave them my eyes!
-Do you call exile a strange place? I call the divided homeland alienation.
Since then the days were passing the same; the bodies were floating in the water, approaching me and trying to touch me, and as I tried to escape to my old days, he appeared on a kite.
Ali is the last type of man I imagined getting attracted to.
He asked if I wanted to abandon the ship and see the place from above.
-From "the above"?
-Yes, Dr. Muhammad, see the whole picture from above, from which God looks at us.
- May God Forgive you!
- Understand me, God is fair, aren't they?
I said yes
- Ok, do you understand why all this ruin is happening? What is the reason, and what is the wisdom behind all these?!
-I do not know.
-Come on, and I'll show you.
I flew with him over the kite. I watched the sea move away and get smaller, becoming a small glass of water filled with corpses and gray dots. I said to myself: We will drink this water one day.
Yes, our bodies will be formed from the bodies of those who left.
They remain here in us; in the soul is a memory and in the body as life.

I flew over all countries. I heard the sounds of crying, laughter, screaming, lullabies of joy and mourning!

I heard backbiting and gossip. I heard encouragement and praise.

I flew over dance places, houses of worship, schools, and amusement parks.

I flew over the airports and watched millions leave and millions return.

I heard newborns' first cries and the commandments' last words.

The scene was complete and solemn, and when he turned to Alis's ivory shoulders, he wasn't there, and I woke up.

****

Nigma was Heba's only refuge after the ordeal of her imprisonment. She visits her daily; she never talks about what happened and doesn't ask Heba to say anything.

She comes every evening after work, cleans the house, cooks, and asks Heba to eat with her.

- I don't have any appetite.

-You don't like my cooking, huh?

Heba eats, then Nigma jumps and fills the place in the beloved Tunisian dialect:

-When you need a translator for my accent, tell me.

Heba smiles in gratitude.

Actually, Heba did not hear more than ten percent of Najma's words. Her mind was still clouded by the impact of the jailer's steps and a painful question: Why? Why do bad things happen to good people?

After about two months, Heba became more and more of a listener to Nigma.

on an April evening, she asked her:

Nigma, I want to visit Tunisia. Will you take me?

Nigma hesitated a little:

- I will take you, but in the future, I was thinking of a visit to the mother of the World. What do you think?

-Egypt?

- Yes, Egypt.

-Yes, when?

-As quickly as possible. What do you say you write while I prepare for travel?

-Write?

Heba thought, why not write books for children like the Danish Hans Christian Andersen ones?

Why don't you open a publishing house for Iraqi children, our hope?

Why don't you give hope to children if giving it to adults has a very high price in this land of horrors?

She needs advice from a promising publishing house in Egypt; she got to know its owner through virtual space. So, when Nigma suggested visiting Egypt for the first time after the bitter prison experience, Heba breathed hope.

Nigma came out on that day very happy, for Hiba, who was rejected by the majority in her ordeal and dwelled in depression, is getting healed and wants to travel.

She remembered a famous saying: "every person in this life fights a painful battle, so do not cause him to be killed."

Nigma wept; the sky in Iraq knows our battles, and if we forget to continue, we will perish.

On the corner of the road, she saw two girls, one of them said:

-Could you please take a picture of us?

Nigma replied:

-Of course.

The girls smiled, and Iraq lived for a moment in their smiles.

- I wish I could take her to Tunisia. I wish I had a better family and I didn't have to run away. Oh Lord, please help us.

****

When they told Ali that all the regions were "mugged," he did not know what this meant.

He had little hope in his heart about a tomorrow that would not stifle his children's future with hatred.

Some loyalists looted houses with the kidnapping captives by some in the opposition; there was no longer any room for doubt that the country had opened the gates of the earthly Hell.

This Hell does not resemble fire in anything. Instead, it kills you without touching you: it kills your children's future and the security of your dreams. It kills your and your neighbor's abilities to share the pain, and when people don't understand others' pain become, at best, enemies. For Ali, Syria was his mother and father. He wrote to me that day: "The homeland is more precious in the heart of orphans, as we buried our loved ones in its land. I feel that I am very orphaned and without a homeland."

- Sorry to read this, when are you coming back?
- Not until I bring another Jasmine, or maybe the same girl, I don't know. The important thing is that she is a seven-year-old girl. They told me that her name was Jasmine too. Maybe after they learned that ISIS took the little girl Yasmine, who I was looking for.
This poor child - whatever her name - moves from one house to another, with no one left for her.
- And when will you bring her?
- After entering the borders of "Abu Tha'laba Al-Taghlibi" Emirate.
- Kidding, huh?
- No, this is his name, his origin is Jordanian, but he decided to wage jihad from here and rid the Islamic nation.
Ali laughed.
- So, you were joking about trying to enter his emirate, huh?!
-No, I am not joking, I will grow a beard, and soon I will be "Abu Qahhar Al-Idlibi."
-What is this name? For God's sake, are you speaking seriously?
-Of course, can you imagine that I enter the name of Nietzsche or even Ali?
-I never want you to enter this emirate. Do you know what it means to catch you?
-Haha, I don't want to know.
Then he sent me a smiley face.
-You reduced your attacks against "Muslims"; did they threaten you?
-You mean my trials to criticize reality, yet make some youth use their brains?
-What is the difference?

-Big difference! Criticism is conscious, shedding light on mistakes because you want to change for the better.

The attack is our weapon against wolves; if they assault us, you know they have no brains.

If an intellectual born in a Muslim environment attacks Islam as a whole and considers all Muslims to be terrorists, why do we write?

-I did not understand you?

- I mean, if you, as an intellectual born in a Muslim environment, attack all Muslims, first you neglect those who think like you among Muslims. Secondly, how will your words be heard among them? They won't read a line. So if you want to change, a kind sermon is the best.

- I will take you to the Emirate of "Al Taghlibi." You argue wisely!

****

The dream of the kite and the repercussions of other ships haunted me for months afterward. At the same time, the news of the Syrian destruction occupied the western news.

I continue to think about his question:

- Ok, understand why all this ruin is happening. What is the reason, and what is the wisdom?

He's right: Why are we all halves?

Why are we all without the security of a homeland?

-Why do we need to beg for our rights?

Why did we lose the war?

All of us, yes, all of us.

We all lost the war with all our political, religious, and social sects.

What victory as we turn into numbers on ships in a raging ocean of corpses?!

What is the reason, and what is the wisdom?

-As for a reason I do not fully know, perhaps injustice. Perhaps hatred, Sectarianism, Politicians' use of saints, Preferring full pockets over full hearts.

As for wisdom:

When the country is devoid of freedom of expression when thinking becomes forbidden, hate penetrates people's hearts, blasphemy becomes a religion, and religion becomes an alienation.

11- Peoples of Metonymy!

God does not dwell in gold houses but lives in golden hearts.
And gold is the best in us:
Poverty made it
Humiliate the injustice forced us to create it
The crowns marginalized it
And when beards raped our dreams
We used our "gold."
The gold in us is the great house of God
Not what is restricted by lineage
The few make a pilgrimage to it
Hear the voice of God in what we sacrificed
While the majority follow tradition and commons
And pay the money to roam the old stone
If Muhammad had lived again
He'll burn the precious things of your idols
Sell what you call the furnishings of the houses of God
To cover the nakedness of your dens.
I wrote this in the virtual space before Ahlam started her inspiring chat
with me:
-How can we see the truth?
-Well, I'll refer you to another piece I wrote last year:
In simple glimpses of this life lies the whole secret:
In the theft of worshipers' shoes
 In the beheading of a woman who dared to reason
 In losing a friend to a political dispute
In immigration search for a homeland

in your need for a stranger to help
in reviving memories
In recreating old stories
In death
in love
In cruelty
in softness
In faith, yes, in faith
In simple glimpses, you see the entire face of the truth, and the truth
does not show its full face unless it stings!
- Great one, you use beautiful metonymy.
- We are the people of metonymy. I do not know why we turned to
disgrace and reproach.
****

In the time of atonement, thinking became forbidden to the human mind,
and the fields of accusation in the name of God expanded until they
filled the future of the simple with terrorism. Hence, the youth became
haunted by the obsession with sex. Development became a dream
subject to the control of beards.
The Arabs were pushed back to the most despicable age, and harassment
spread, rape, severing of the necks, the possession of the queens of the
right, and the spread of forbidden, suspicious shameless, and vulgar
relationships.
The name of the era is concealment, not piety.
In the light of all this, those who forbade metaphors for writers and pen
holders appeared!
The (Muslims) forgot that their book is based on metaphors.
 Per history, it was revealed to the Arabs because the Arabic language
bears and is beautified by metaphors and allegories.
This is the tip of the iceberg; The "story of ISIS" iceberg.
The deep mountain in the culture contains the story of selling ignorance
to hungry people and giving them bread for beards, unfair analysis of
history, and crowns' interpretations of the Qur'an.

If the Arabs want to survive, they must resort to real scholars, those who have studied the Arabic language and delved into the art of metonymy and metaphor. Only then would religion return to the conscience and mind of our youth instead of being an indisputable inheritance.

I had no news about Ali for days, and his memories became more than I could bear.

On a sunny holiday morning, I entered my new house, which now had big and broad windows; I looked at Jose:

-Thanks, you're talented.

He blushed:

-Thank you, doctor. He answered me in beautiful, broken English.

-All we have left is the floor and the kitchen.

-As for the kitchen, I want it white, its large window overlooking the garden, and they share a stone stand together.

We will put a marble on it, and it will become a table. Thus the marble of the sink in the kitchen extends to the garden.

-Can you explain to me a little more, I don't think I understood how you want the wall?

- We transform the upper wall between the kitchen and the garden into a large window that opens fully.

The marble sink in the kitchen overlooking this window will resemble a table extending from the kitchen to the garden.

Friends sit inside or outside according to their desire, but their marble table is one, and the delivery becomes Easier to bring food back to the kitchen.

-The large, hinged window will help in that; I mean, the kitchen marble next to the sink extends beyond the window to the garden.

I understand.

- Yes, Jose, you are talented, and this will be easy for you.

As I was speaking to Jose, I received a friend request from "Abu Qahar Al-Idlibi."

I remembered that Ali mentioned this name to use in the emirate he decided to enter.

I quickly returned home and entered the page. I saw it was completely empty, the account was new, and this is mostly the Syrian.

I accepted the request and waited two hours before receiving his message in English:
"Tomorrow, I leave for the land of Hamza. I have three dreams.".
Then the account was deleted.
****

Heba, who owes a lot to Nigma, saw a mutual interest in living together. Thus, safety spread in the air of the room, and the painful memories diminished.

Heba's place was not big; it was a studio.

Her hope for a house in this country is similar to the hope for Arab unity.

Then there was a room, then two rooms with a permanent change of residence so that the hand of darkness does not reach her address again.

What justice surrounds the imagination homes we emigrate to live in?

With this and that, Heba returned to life; she came back to light up Ammar's sky with her discussions and fill the Baghdadi evenings with tranquility.

-The person who invented the calendar was very clever. Humans are by nature bored, most of them forget, and most of them need new imaginary beginnings.

-As few know, the beginning occurs every morning and with every sunrise. Few also remember the favor and do not deny those who helped and supported them.

 Scarcity remembers you in your ordeal and keeps your secrets in your absence.

- The issue is more complicated than this. Look at the people around you. They gather around each other for joy, and when the actual bell of need rings, they disappear. Their subconscious invents reasons. So, you find material help becomes a dream, and moral assistance is forgotten.

- I'm afraid I have to disagree with you here; the majority of people are absent when they feel weak or depressed or, at best, due to sadness and distress.

 An absent person is a person who needs us. He needs support, reassurance, and perhaps a simple question:

-Do you need me? This question is the "Happy New Year."
The actual sentence, not the repeated false one. As for the current social obligation. Iraq is going into a revolution.
- This is what I meant, the golden sentence in relationships:
 I do not want you only to be happy, but I welcome your sadness before your joy. Your weakness before your strength, your requests before your gifts. I know that you are a human being, not an angel. I am not an angel, either. Please tell me when you need me.
  In the new year, don't curse it. Mornings are different, with different dreams.
Do you need me, friend? Cheer up: Iraq to a revolution!

12- The land of Coincidences

I imagine a tree instead of the tombstone of every grave in this world; How beautiful would the graves look? How common will visiting cemeteries become? We would have the hug of our loved ones again, and we will be hugged one day!

In the last stages of cancer, the cells of the body begin to succumb to the cancerous cells gradually.

Immunity continues to get weakened until the barriers against pathogens also break down.

Some people do not give up and resist stubbornly, and we see recovery cases that medicine cannot explain. In other cases, the body is sacked by diseases, so the soul leaves to a better place.

Many believe that the other place is another living body: a person, an animal, a flower, or a tree!

Changing the culture of cemeteries may create better perspectives.

Changing human interaction with cemeteries may imprint the culture of an entire people and raise us from the ranks of third-world places in many ways.

Tombs are not only outside our bodies; we may also carry them in us, plant a tree, and live after your death!

****

Ammar came out not knowing where to go; his heart was crying while his eyes insisted not to. People on strange roads were swift, and he was still pulling his heart cart.

The doctor diagnosed him with depression. He laughed: you mean, I'm crazy.

The doctor said: This is the old stigma of psychiatric illness. Now they display that a lack of serotonin causes depression.

-Sero? What? What did you say? Do you mean I have to walk*?

The doctor smiled, and Ammar, from that day, was walking.

He crossed the whole city:

He passed by the quail shop Abu Mazen, turned his face so as not to greet him, he heard his voice:

-Mr. Ammar, please remember your dept.

He owns Abu Mazen fifty thousand. Do you know what fifty thousand means? -he asked himself, and his mind answered:

-Fifty thousand lumps in the morsel, drenched in humiliation.

He passed by Souad's house, and Souad, who repeated the stories of the hareem*, left him for a close friend.

She didn't live here anymore; Bahia, the dancer, occupied the house.

Bahia threw her anklets at him with a red message. The important thing was that he did not defile the place; this is what he convinced himself with.

He passed by his manager's car and saw him kissing one of the female employees. She wasn't the secretary - he said to himself - some people in this east don't kiss the secretary.

He arrived at a road bend, and on one side, there was a bridge that suggested a bloody idea that had been circulating in his mind for a long time, a frightening, horrible idea.

He thought: It is an infidel, a criminal and murderous to those around him, a defeated and poisonous idea; yes, he thought of committing suicide.

He said to himself:

-Why not?

Then he decided to take the other side and think about it more.

His steps began to accelerate in the opposite direction, asking himself:

Why do I exist in this life?

How do I cope?

Why did she leave me?

Why did he betray me?

Why did I fail?

Why did I collapse like the shadow of a light bulb used for torture?

Why didn't Heba love me? And Abeer trampled my heart?

He resolved that there was no other solution; the white bridge was hanging in his memory as a homeland now.

His feet were preparing to return while a small hand pulled his brown coat.

-I want Mommy.

A four-year-old girl, her face is an authentic Iraqi brown, the honey of her beauty mixes with the gold of her innocent and frightened eyes. Her clothes are old but clean.

-Where is your mother, little one?

-At home, then she started crying.

Ammar carried the little girl

 - Don't be afraid, my child; we'll find Mommy today.

****

The child told him that her name was Tota. She did not know more.

Ammar carried her to the police station in the area.

They told him: You can leave her and go, thank you, we will take care of the matter; he did not accept.

He waited with her for six hours. He bought her a cheese sandwich and sweets, fed her, and did not leave her even for a second.

Then he waited another two hours and was about to argue with the police about taking her to Heba's house.

When Baghdad came, a woman in her thirties, thin and pale in an old long black dress and masculine torn shoes.

Despite her beauty, sadness radiated from her face like a fulfilled wish that had come true so late, her eyes were exhausted, and her hair was thick, black, and plaited.

She hugged the child, and they both cried.

Thank you for saving Tota, Taima, my child. They pulled her from my hand in a crowdy farmers' market. I searched and cried all day. You saved me, too; I was thinking of jumping off the white bridge tonight.

-The white bridge? Tonight?

Ammar's heart and mind stopped for a split second.

It could not be true. This is like a poorly directed old Indian or Arabic movie.

He had lost faith in the unseen and souls for a long time. He stood in astonishment with his mouth wide open.

-God bless you. God gives you until he pleases you. You saved two souls, Tota and me; give me your hand, let me kiss it.

Your deed is on my head all life; I will never forget what you did; I appreciate you, and may God protect you.

Ammar finally smiled and told the grateful lady:

-He protected me; believe me, God protected me.

"We are in this place and this hour for a purpose. No matter how much we fail, no matter how many slaps and disappointments we have, what we were created for is coming, and it will not be simple no matter how we think it is.

Today is the birthday that I chose: Happy new life to me.

Ammar wrote this message to "Heba" from over the white bridge while finally allowing his eyes to cry.

****

At the same time and in a different place:

Heba repeatedly wrote Ammar's name on a white sheet of paper; after writing it, she would put the Arabic accent on it and then change it into Heba's name.

She knows that she has stood again. It is like a tree that threw its seeds to the ground before being burned.

Something died in her; however, many bushes filled the place, and young versions of Heba's strength gave her voices instead of one and allowed her to live many lives.

The Iraqi Heba was once destroyed by being a detainee accused of insulting the religion and the country inequitably.

Heba returned to life and stood as bright as the sun. Her articles filled Arab websites and social media pages.

She evaded prosecution by changing her address every three months.

Ammar knew how to find her, and she is now seeing his strong presence in her life—not only feeling his attention.

-"What is between us is beyond love."

This is what he said to her, and she is still thinking about it.

It amazed her, and she was an eccentric not to refuse this man. And it surprised her that she turned to him whenever she was sad.

He convinced her that the person who gave you the most in this life is the one who gave you the ability to be persistent, the ability to continue, and never give up!

****

-What ugliest than the assassination of laughs?

How hard it is to see an arrow piercing your soul. Plugging it, then burying a piece of it in the cemetery of your heart.

Love is the main element missing in the last stages of any mental illness. No end-stage psychiatric illness can happen unless the person completely misses the amulets of love.

-I am a psychiatrist, and I don't understand. Could you please explain this to me?

-There is no resistant illness if love spells around the patient, love from a mother, father, relative, friend's heart, or any flowering heart.

-I am not sure how to interpret this philosophy into medicine.

- No need; keep it philosophical:

In the heart of each of us are graves of love's memories, failed goals, pains we blocked, and others' acts that assassinated our laughter in many moments; let all go and go on!

-If you decide to surrender and build stones over "the graves," then ignore their occurrence and continue with your life, trying to guard your "cemetery" so no one enters it or illuminates any of its memories.

But if you give psychiatry a key to your life, then love will grow above the graves in your heart; like a tree that embraces the soul, you'll dream again.

There is no mental illness that eats you unless you accept the role of the "cemetery guard" don't do it, please change it into a garden, then let it go, and never give up!

****

Diyar and Abeer entered Iraq the same day "the Syrian" entered!
The coincidences that we hear about in legends are a great truth.
Similar souls meet one day in one or another life!
At the airport, they told them:
"All Syrians, please wait here; the procedures for stamping your
passports are slightly different; we apologize.
No one in that group had a Syrian passport except Ali and Abeer.
They sat beside each other while Diyar went to get his passport stamped.
Abeer heard Ali talking to the three children about the reason for these
procedures; then, he asked them to sleep until the wait ended.
Abeer smiled:
-You reminded me of my mother; she always said to go to sleep when
confused about something.
Ali laughed:
- How sweet! Typical Syrian mother! I am Ali; what is your name?
-Abeer.
- A common beautiful Syrian name. Do you live in Iraq now?
-I used to live in Lebanon, and it is my first-time entering Iraq; I'll try to
get work here.
- In which city?
-Baghdad.
- I am also going with my children to Baghdad, my friends are there.
-Do you want to share one big car?
- Sure, it would be conducive.
In the meantime, Diyar returned, and a friendly conversation took place
between the three of them!

130

13- We Sell Hope!

The countries were lost between the regimes and their opposition. And youth stood at the gates of embassies and the work "famines." Some people came out calling to heal a large wound, dividing the country into two halves without stitches?

Everyone said I was not the culprit.

While we, as strangers, leaked out the wound, invisible, flexible red blood cells.

Black bearded germs entered with their black flag and fearsome reputation.

The wound got bigger.

Poverty grew pus

Hatred made it numb

Then you asked why the homeland would not stand?

Because after his children leaked out

The "homeland had anemia."

And because the germs had reached the bone

Threatened permanent paralysis

You asked:

-Why do you hate the opposition and curse the kings?

-Because I am a flexible red blood cell that ran away into a real homeland!

****

What is your favorite holiday in America?

-Thanksgiving.

- What's its story?

-People gather all over the United States to thank God for "his" many blessings. Many stories behind it, but the mutual element is gratitude.

- This is beautiful. I wonder how it has not reached Arab countries. We have imported a lot of holidays.

- Some families celebrate it, Ahlam. My family used to celebrate it.
-Maybe because you have traveled a lot.
The Thanking there that I know:
Arab governments "thank" their minds by arresting them because of their humane difference.
Or that the tyrannical regimes "thank" their youth who remained in the homelands by killing them. Because of their demand for the right to decent education, dignity, and stability of a homeland!
- Revolutionary Ahlam! You are now here under American law. No worries! Also, a new hope was raised, and the Iraqi revolution became apparent.
-Do you think they will do it?
-Necessarily.
-Connect me to the (Facebook) pages that called for the revolution in Iraq; I want to drink from the same hope!
- You got it, Ahlam!
****

-Even if I'll get charcoal for my extensive hard work, I will never give up.
To stop digging in this life means surrendering to death.
-Are you still thinking about the children's publishing house?
- Yeah, what do you think?
-Isn't a kindergarten for orphans and special needs children make a better idea?
-Maybe, but it needs more money.
- We can rely on donations. The important thing is to obtain licenses. This may happen if Nigma helps us by virtue of her current work in the Ministry of Education.
-I'll ask her. I can write and publish on Facebook, it is in every house, and I do not write for fame.
-Fame is essential; otherwise, how will your writing reach as many children as possible?
-The religious references here - as you know-put my name on the lists of the infidels.

135

-Go ahead and apologize to them.

-About what, Ammar? I didn't do anything wrong. On the contrary, I am a victim of the regime. And these religious "authorities" did nothing to help me.

There is no place for religious "kingdoms" at this time. They must fight poverty, injustice, and discrimination before they brag and show us the ways of faith.

-Heba, I understand what you mean, and I know that you are not against them, but their deification while they are human beings who make mistakes like us. I know that you want us to be governed by a just law that applies to everyone and equals everyone, however, your expressions are harsh, and you may be misunderstood again.

- I don't care; you believe the solution is through them, and I see the solution through science and reason, far away from the religious "kings."

-I understand that you want the people of knowledge to take over the reins, each in his field.

The doctor in medicine, the teacher in the school, the engineer in the construction, and the Sheikh* in the mosques.

But the simple people need someone to represent them under a religious framework; believe me, after they have lost everything, they need daily assurance that God sees and knows what they suffered.

- And I am not against this, but against asking a journalist to become a sycophant, and instead of the press's duty to shed light on all mistakes, the press has red lines under the - incorrect interpretations - of the clergy.

The place of religious references should not be with the regimes. Permitting the influence and interference of religious parties in the civil state and the decisions of individuals is wrong. Instead, they should appeal to reason and support science.

I support the Abrahamic religion.

-What is this?

-A religion unites the three monotheistic religions: Judaism, Christianity, and Islam. Putting all together is the same religion will participate in solving the middle east's malignant conflicts.

- I am afraid about your safety Heba. I understand your faith and wisdom, but some people understand half of the words and analyze half of the speech. I told you Iraq would go into a revolution. Now, look how we started with the demonstrations, women and men, under one flag of Iraq! Heba, wait for us to win.

-Maybe we need a homeland in which we are not afraid of paying the price of difference. I am worried about revolutions that will be ruled partly by the authority of males and the stick of history.

 I do not mean to discourage you, but with all my pain, I am fearful of the revolution. I fear for our youth, as many of them have been taught the culture of death.

We must invent a way to glorify the art of life; this will only happen by separating religion from the state.

Ammar wanted to hug Heba. He hesitated, then approached shyly. He put his arm on her shoulder; she put her hand on his:

-Agreed, he said. And with a big hug:

-I love you, Heba.

****

In her last look at Palmyra - with the handcuffs around her wrists - Zenobia's* body language said what the legends of Rome and the wonders of history had not.

"Zenobia" stood lofty and majestic, mocking those who consider women a commodity that requires covering or stripping.

Everyone forgot Aurelian's face, who arrested Zenobia and almost forgot his name. Yet, at the same time, the glory of women's rule remained pulsating in the ruins of Palmyra, and the confident, unencumbered body language remained in the paintings of the creators.

I taught the residents I teach in psychiatry the art of body language from films and descriptions in international novels.

Body language tells you everything you want to know about a person.

In body language, love reveals its silence, and hate reveals the meaning of the enemy.

I became known as the doctor who hears the sound of your silence, and psychiatry is still my eternal message.

I tried to spread the culture of fighting stigma in the Arab countries after discovering dopamine, serotonin, noradrenaline, and other chemical messengers. How can a sane person believe in madness?

What do sorcery and witchcraft have to do with treating mental illness? Each of us has a disease that will reach him sooner or later.

It could be Vitiligo, Depression, Bipolar, Psoriasis, Pemphigus, Acne vulgaris, Hypertension, Cancer, Diabetes, Schizophrenia, Anxiety, and many more.

Some skin diseases are similar to psychological disorders; All are similar to patience. They can't be caused by one single definitive reason, and they are not contagious diseases.

So, let us learn to look into the eyes and understand the smile before judging people.

In psychiatry, we sell hope. That is why you, as a doctor, have to be a professional with optimism. And more than that, an artist in spinning and making hope.

Otherwise, "Who does not have a thing cannot give it," And your work will lose much of its meaning.

My humble work is like a hummingbird; I never wanted my achievements to prey and grow like eagles or swarm to gain glory like flocks!

I always wanted it to sound like a hummingbird, yeah, that little bird. The hummingbird is tiny in size - unnoticed - by many.

It is the wisest bird and can control its flight. It flies forward and backward if needed. It also passes vertically, but it knows that the peaks are only stations.

The hummingbird's brain works fidelity and always remembers the favor, enabling him to remember every flower he visited.

Gratitude is the essence of nobles, gratitude to everyone who helped me, and praise and thanks be to God for everything.

This was what I said to myself after I hung Zenobia's painting, and now my home is ready to be entered.

My house looks much more extensive than its actual size, and if I put my furniture in it, it will fit perfectly.

I don't want to think about the Syrian; my " Superego"* supports what he did, while my " Id"* asks me every day:
 Why did he sell you? And how did he replace it with an imaginary future with your three children? So, you became the spinster waiting for someone who might never return.
I remembered that I got used to the losses in heart wars. I am the lady of failed hearts' battles. No one is better than me at attracting sad endings. On another wall in the house is a painting in beautiful Arabic script: "You are what you dream of being."
By: Lama Muhammad
My golden sentence! The painting was given to me by Kamal. - my old imaginary "love"- in our golden age.
I remembered Kamal and his reproach to me with the legitimacy of masculinity:
"You are too strong and rebellious; you need a man to tame you."
This is what he said when I opposed his political opinion, and it was the last thing I allowed him to " vomit."
My respect for myself is the master of all situations; I will not allow any male to snipe that.
I am as I dream of being. He is married and miserable in his marriage as in his work today.
The diversity of the contents of my house makes it a simple museum of my travels and beliefs.
Here in the corner is a large painting of white swans. It was painted after the Swan Lake ballet by Tchaikovsky, but I bought it because it reminded me of the origin of the fairytale when the princes shapeshifter from human form to swan forms by a curse, yet their beloved sister needed to make them sweaters from the nettle's plants.
The sister was required to continue to be silent till she was done, and for me, it meant more than silence; it meant calmly seeing the whole truth.
How can I get rid of the curse that affected a whole country? The full truth bled my hands, and I lost many semi-friends. The easier way to lose people is to tell them the entire truth.

With the deterioration of the Syrian economy and the spread of unemployment and poverty, hatred is still the leading cause of the curse that afflicted that land.

Unfortunately, the partisans do not wear nettles, even if it carries their salvation.

What do we have to do, y' Alia - I told myself-

-The first dinner will be "Freekeh*," and the first to be invited are Umniah, Nile, and Ahlam.

As for the first song in the house, it would be with Fayrouz, Ali Badr Al-Din, the Rahbani brothers with Maqam Al-Hijaz:

- I have neither land nor housing, "my dreams" are my homeland.

****

Today's demonstrations in Iraq have become the talk of the world.

Young men and women of the age of flowers worked together in cleaning streets and old buildings.

They planted flowers in the deserted streets, as hope is in the hearts of millions.

The Iraqi flag brought them together, and they did not allow any entry to any other flag.

They painted beautiful paintings on old walls and gave them lives.

They renounced sectarianism. They carried their hopes for a homeland.

Yes, their motto was "We Want a Homeland."

As for the best means of transportation, there was the auto-rickshaw.

It is called the tuk-tuk in Iraq, and it is a vehicle (motorcycle) with three wheels. The driver sits in the front, and two passengers are in the back, or three at some times. It solved a transportation crisis in some countries around the world.

Its drivers in the Iraq revolution had many stories of chivalry and helping others.

The tuk-tuk symbolized the brave Arab revolutions; it looked more like our hope for our right not to be expatriated, for our right to live with dignity in our homelands.

The country that chases ideas is a giant prison; the "homeland" that besieges thinking is occupied no matter how some try to beautify the ugly picture.

The Iraqi youth did not try to beautify the picture; instead, they tried to draw a new vision of a homeland that would include us all.

-We are looking for a house, now we share rooms in a student house.

-Student house?

-Yes, a big house, his owner rents rooms for students. I rented a space for the children and me. Diyar rented a room for himself and another one for Abeer.

-Is Abeer still helping you?

- Very, you can say that she adopted children.

A stupid female feeling of jealousy stirred in me:

-Does she have time? You told me she works as a nurse, right?

- She has no time except for Diyar and the children. She cooks large quantities to share with us. Diyar helps put the children into school in the morning; we own him, along with a journalist here, in getting the children to school quickly.

I noted my stupid longing feelings:

- You are lucky to have them all; I hope to get to know them.

- Hope for that too. Please consider coming to visit here.

- Are you staying that long? When are you coming back?

-Not until I find my mother's family and know how to take the children with me to America.

-You are a Syrian American citizen, and you can't bring them?

-Unfortunately, it is not that easy, and the cost of living in America with kids is higher than I expected.

Ali told me also that Hamza helped him find a temporary job as an engineer in a company. Then, he met a journalist trying to open kindergartens for war orphans—the same one who helped Diyar get the children into school—

- She came to me while I was trying to get birth certificates for the children and told me about her project.

Her name is Heba, she does not have a permanent address now, but she comes to the Civil Registration department to meet people trying to help children who are victims of wars.

She will help me get birth certificates. The situation here is just like Syria.

I said to myself: Heba too!

Then told him:

- God blessed you and the children with Heba too. Iraq is similar to Syria in everything, and it resembles every Arab country with people's kindness and willingness to help children unconditionally.

The speech about disease, chaos, fanaticism, nepotism, and immigration blames Syria for Iraq and all Arab countries.

With the spread of the legitimate right to revolution, and the lack of silence about injustice, hope has embraced the youth's dreams of destroying idols and advancing homelands.

Ali wrote:

Speaking of hope:

-I miss you, Alia, so much.

I smiled when I saw the last sentence:

- Me too.

I wrote it, then erased it, and wrote:

-I miss you, Syrian hero!

It is said that the survivors of wars suffer from an overwhelming sense of guilt, the survivor's guilt.

It is also said that jealousy resides in survivors' hearts, and they envy people who stayed in their homelands and weren't forced to abandon their memories.

This abundance of feelings is the most beautiful thing that can be imagined about the human soul.

That is why we find in the literature of alienation of courage and beauty what is not in other literature.

The idea of the revolution of the Iraqi youth revived in me great hope in change, in their ability to return the homelands stolen by the "religious" merchants, the kings, and the politicians.

The prophecy is still eternal that the return of Iraq's minds is a prelude to the return of all middle east countries.

My heart is still without limits

A mind without frames

A soul without the shackles of hatred

So, dreams know no despair, and goals are waiting there.

I continued my work in the garden of my new home. In the left corner, I placed a model of a hummingbird in the colors: Green, white, red, black, and blue.

Gardenia and jasmine are planted in the herbaceous garden paths.

And in the right corner of the garden, I put a small hammock to catch me when tears filled the place.

Love is still my master and king after God.

14- "Do Not Be Sad; God is With Us."

The generation of the nineties
 The posterity of hope and revolutions
The globalization generation
 The internet
And personal newspapers!
The posterity of "Where did you get this from?"
Instead of pharisaism
The generation of love
Victorious of love
Over the turmoil of sects and the pavilion of nationalities
The courage after generations of cowardice
Setbacks
Calamities
And disappointments.
Age of rocks supports our dreams after the generations of the parties
sold us the slogans. After shameful ongoing girls' infanticides
This generation is our hope and the nightmare of dictatorships!
Heba's article was filling the websites:
"I love you, Baghdad.
Kings thank the rats of the sultans for giving them the authority in
nipping the books of writers and skipping over the "cheese" of the
simple.
I thank God for the blessing of mind's cats with seven lives!
They will not stop thinking until catching the last rat.
Praise be to God before and after:
"Do not be sad; God is with us."
****

Ammar did not know that his prophecy about the Iraqi revolution would
become true.
The injustice, humiliation, poverty, and nepotism inflicted a curse on the
government.

Iraqi youth filled the streets, without sectarian affiliations or ethnic classifications, under one flag, the Iraqi flag.

In the era of globalization, how can any government steal its people? How can an official brag about his money when it has no source but the pockets of the simple?

Every evening, Ammar counted his dreams as stars in the sky of the liberation revolution, Iraq was revolting, and God was with him.

-If there is God, they would be with humanism, not sectarianism, nor partisanship. God would never prefer a country over a country or a group of people over others.

- I am afraid, Ammar, that the government will not like this situation, so it insists on reversing the facts. Therefore, it issues gangs with the masks of revolution.

- Do not be afraid; no people read like the Iraqi people; there is no place for sectarianism here.

- This is an oil country. Those who covet it wish for civil war. The civil war in the Arab countries is one of the keys to safety for the western economy.

- No worries, the Iraqis are conscious due to the many past conspiracies.

-Some hate the revolution, and some want to live, and I don't blame them.

-The people who most hate revolutions are those who deep down want to participate in them.

But they are ruled by fear, as happened in Syria before Islamization stole any torch for a revolution.

And before sectarianism allowed any hope for a future for all.

Here the youth rose under one flag.

Do you know what happens when the youth rise with the support of the sky?

Even if the change is delayed, it is definitely coming!

- No comment on beautiful beginnings, Ammar; all beginnings are beautiful.

A bad prophecy destroys any victory without justice and any revolution whose supporters think they are defending religion.

Religion defends people with the help of law, not the other way around.

Therefore, the revolution that does not separate religion from politics, and is not framed by the struggles of history, frightens me greatly.
-The Iraqi youth are mostly conscious and mature.
- Sorry, Ammar. The dire prophecy tells of upcoming devastation; it is sad to share this now. Talking about it is like making the mother owl: Wise but fearful.
- As for me, I am optimistic and happy; the Iraqi people before the revolution are unlike them after it.
****

The bet at this time is only on your will.
The stake is in our insistence on dreaming and challenging circumstances without losing ourselves in the middle of the road.
The only loser is the one who does not believe in their own priorities, power, and abilities, in God's spirit in them.
The only loser is the person who leaves his goals and doesn't believe that the sky protects real dreams.
Other than that, we are little stories that will end on a very ordinary day.
I wrote this on my Facebook page before the Syrian message arrived to reassure me about him and his children.
He wrote jokingly:
-We are fine. It seemed that every time I entered a place, the revelation started.
-Haha, I think so.
Then I wrote:
-The Iraqi revolution is an inevitable result of what happened in that beautiful country over the past two decades.
They have the right to live with dignity; the noblest and bravest young people can't find work, and many children are without the minor conditions of satisfaction in obtaining their right to study.
 Women under the whip of puritanism.
 Writers and poets are stigmatized as infidels for not accepting associating partners with God and for not deification the owners of crowns and turbans.
What do we have to do? Immigrate or protest, no other solution!

-You are right; the people are not stupid.
Globalization is not in the interest of the regimes or their lining.
-Did you find a home?
- I will not change my residence now.
- Are you thinking of coming back?
- To America?
- Yes, you have someone waiting for you here.
- Transferring children is complex, and I need a lawyer to help me.
After the revolution here, many state departments are down.
- How are Yasmine, Omar and Raqqa?
-Angels. Jasmine has a lot of nightmares, so Abeer takes her at night and puts her on her lap.
- Noble Abeer.
-Very, even though Jasmine told her the story, she didn't tell me or hint that she knew they are not my children. It will be difficult for Jasmine to leave her.
- How is Diyar?
- Fine. He works as an Arabic language teacher. Now with schools closed, he works as a cook for young people in Tahrir Square*.
Ali and I were chatting - as usual - through the chat window on Facebook; however, I could hear the voice of his concern.
Ali is questioning his decision to adopt children. He has enough guilt complexes to kill many hopes.
As a psychiatrist, I am accustomed to not relying on any diagnostic analysis in my relationships, and although the profession often impresses you, I am still good at the art of playing dumb.
-Things will get better, don't worry.
- I hope the Arab countries are united in misfortune that will not change until we get out of the limited inheritance into God's space.
I got disconnected. With the middle eastern curse, we don't get the blessing of saying "goodbye" or "I love you" as a farewell word.
I continue to plant flowers in the garden of my house.
I imagine if I planted them in the streets of Baghdad or Damascus. What would happen in this world if we preserved our right to keep memories and beloved ones. Isn't it one of the simplest human rights?

150

****

-You do not like me.

- I love you, Heba.

-If you love me, why are you protesting? My mind tells me we'll only get humiliation and death.

-I can't believe you're saying that.

- In fact, I know the meaning of imprisonment and humiliation, and above it, I know the meaning of countries ruled by groups, religious in the outward, but the inner is political.

-Religious references and parties are with us and protect us.

- This is strange, Ammar. Strange. This is the opposite of what logic and reason say. How can we revolt under the condition of loyalty to anyone except God? How do we give our right to think to anyone other than our brains?

How can our first demand not be a secular law like the laws of the countries that our youth seek day and night to migrate to?

Why not become like some Western countries in respecting human rights? This is a rich country with history, tourism, gas, and oil; what do we need then?

- Heba, I believe in the goodness of religious references and parties.

- I am not here to interfere with your convictions, but how can I be convinced that what happened in Iraq for so many years was without their knowledge? Why did they remain silent all that time?

-They did not remain silent, but the system was corrupt.

-Any system in the world is corrupt if there is no law governing it, separated from religion, independent of the interests of other countries, and far from the kingdom of sects.

 A law that applies to everyone without exception. The revolution in Arab countries must start with the liberation of minds and religious heritage first; otherwise, we will only have more blood.

-If I had not known your belief in God, I would have said that you are calling to unbelief.

- If I had not known that you are now fascinated by the hope of the revolution. I would have said I did not know you; the revolution needs to demand a just law above all.

Ammar turned and opened the door to leave:

Iraq will be fine, don't worry.

****

On a cold but sunny morning, Umniah knocked on my door.

She looked brighter; her eyes were telling the story of a victory!

-I got a divorce and will return to Saudi Arabia soon.

I was aware of Oqla's repeated betrayals and his mistreatment of this queen, so I embraced her:

-Congratulations, sister, you deserve the best in everything.

-If it wasn't for you, Alia. I would have ended my life, perhaps.

God sent you as a sister and friend when I was alone to the bone.

I threatened Oqla to expose his dishonorable relationship with the wife of his boss at work. I imagine he loves her; it is hard to believe he knows how to love! Anyway, this "love" was in my favor after years of humiliation.

-We should celebrate, come live here.

- Can I stay with you till the divorce transaction is completed?

-Sure, you are more than welcome!

- Thank you, sister; I will file a lawsuit to get half of his property. It is not for the love of money. My priceless life was wasted with him.

- I'm not worried about you, Umniah; you are wise and know what you should do.

- Thank you again; please call Nile and Ahlam. I'll invite you to dinner wherever you want.

-You got it! Congratulations again!

We celebrate the divorce!

Yes, if marriage becomes humiliation. If the husband becomes a stranger and if lying becomes a salt.

15- A House Without a Ceiling: We Call It a Homeland!

The Iraqis only wanted tranquility
They love each other unconditionally
They followed God
Yet, the kings of the sects fought them!
Nothing new
Our book is a book of metaphors and allegories
They wanted dignity
Then they got killed for claiming a homeland!
They said their hope was a lie, a misdemeanor, a felony
Among the Arabs are those who did not care about them
they were waiting for a stage and an end
They did not know yet that the Iraqi revolution also had their salvation
And Iraq - as it has always been - was the first to be saved.
The land of salvation and the beginnings
There is no fear for people who read
It is a shame for anyone to think they are the protectors of a religion
In the law of God, we do not worship idols and do not commit captivity.
****

After several weeks of a peaceful demonstration in Iraq and on a bloody night, they entered. They were called the third party by the regimes.
They killed the unarmed demonstrators.
The hearts of mothers burned for their children, and the crying of loved ones reached the sky.
Some people learn about their children's and loved ones' deaths through pictures in the virtual space. As a result, death has once again become free and accessible in Arab countries.

Ammar was trying to pull out one of the wounded when that knife stabbed him in the middle of his back.

He remembered the white bridge and remembered that since the beginning of the revolution in Iraq, he had forgotten to think of death. Yet now, Mr. Death may have come because he ignored it.

The last thing he heard was a gallant Iraqi voice defending him:

- This is a Syrian who has nothing to do with us. Kill us, leave him. We are Iraqis.

He thought, do they think I'm Syrian? Or are they trying to save me?

Is Abeer's Syrian dialect still imprinting my words, or were ten years in Damascus enough to brand me as a Syrian?

His blood filled the dust around him. Abeer's picture at the beginning of the tunnel of his imagination:

-Do you know why we were born as strangers?

-To be fine.

While Heba calls him from the end of the tunnel:

-You'll be fine; we are together.

****

A friend once asked me:

- What do you want me to pray for you?

-Pray for me that God bless me according to my intention.

After he read one of my books, he told me:

- God has granted you the gift of writing, the splendor of expression, and the courage of the truth. All of this sustenance is according to your pure intention.

And I said to myself:

Perhaps, writing is my livelihood in this time; it is what protects me from depression, surrender, and fear.

That is why I did not and will not use it to polish crowns or wash turbans.

 How do you use God's sustenance in idolatry?

I write daily in my tiny house; there are no homes for women who look like me in Iraq or Syria.

As for my house here, it is missing only the loved ones.

There is nothing in it from the laughter of my relatives, my beloved, and my friends in Syria but auditory hallucinations that sadden and gladden me at the same time that I do not hear them.

My house here has all the comforts and one method of torture called memories.

My dears, I will see you in the other world. I burned my bridges of return when I opposed the regimes of political and religious tyranny, and I also fought their infiltrating opposition.

I paid the tax of my independence with the pain of memories.

Love is my master and my religion.

****

The sound of the phone picked me from the imagination's ocean.

I started my evening talk with the Syrian; Ali is now in the heart of the Iraqi revolution, and the events reached me reliable and documented.

- Consider coming to us; the Iraqi revolution will put us on the map again.

-I wish I have the optimism that illuminates your days, Ali.

-What makes life possible is that firm belief that tomorrow is better than today; we are a hostage that only hope can release.

-My basket is pierced. Hope leaks out of it every day.

- Free him. *Hope does not reside in baskets but in "times."*

The only solution is for women to rule us, the men's opportunity is over, they failed.

He was silent for a while, then added:

- I know that the place is not suitable, but the time is appropriate,

Maybe you don't care to know, but *my hope lives in you. I love you.*

Oh, Syrian! You were forever late, and you spoke on the land of Iraq!

Who told you that the place is not suitable? No place like Baghdad, a pure place to express love.

****

Ammar lost consciousness but ironically continued to hear the conversations around him; it sounds like hearing is the first sense we get in this life and possibly the last to lose, he said to himself.

He was walking in the pain forests with the wound on his back; he grabbed his little hand: Come with me, Mr. Pain, I'll get you distracted. And this conversation was the best pain killer:

- They say that religion is the solution, so we do not dare to object. The guillotine of atonement is in their hands, and they judge us whenever they want.

-We are true believers, and those who feel God fear nothing. We'll continue to speak the whole truth, not half of it, and smash idols.

- They don't care about the truth; they want Iraq's oil. That's why they set the place on fire. They want the people to be divided sectarianly and within the same sect too.

-They will not pass. The different points of view are united only by the love of Iraq.

-I do not fear for this country with such braves. That's what Ammar said to himself while he was between memories and God.

They took him to one of the medical tents with nine other wounded. After several hours, he started to wake up.

He remembered his conversations with Heba. She was right when she told him that she feared revolutions would be controlled in one way or another by religious parties.

- Ammar; The wound is not that bad. Ammar, do you remember me? The last person Abeer imagined that she would help was Ammar.

He looked at her tenderly; his eyes said:

-If I knew that a wound in my back would make me see you. I would have prayed to God that life would complete the stabs in my back so, in the revolution, there would be an orphan hope that I would rise again.

Then he changed his position and extended his right hand:

-what's up, sweetie?

She shook his hand:

-Thank God for your safety.

- Adversity does not kill me, Abeer. It cannot kill me. Do you think that whoever revives hope for the return of the homelands will die? Even if his body parts, he does not die.

Abeer, who fully understood what this revolutionary meant to Ammar, smiled as she responded with a statement she read that day by a brave Iraqi journalist named Heba:
- *Praise be to God before and after:*
"Do not be sad; God is with us."
****

Every evening my sadness sits with me to drink matcha green tea and write for the sake of resurrection. The resurrection of the science in countries that need it.
I imagine my mother drinking her Arabic coffee while sitting quietly in the hammock:
-Today's horoscope: Do not be reckless. Sagittarius, Sagittarius: The most adventurous zodiac, honest and frank, ease it, stop being that kind.
Dad fixes the floor:
- I told you high heels would click this stone, and it's bad for your back too.
My brother sits next to a hummingbird, makes it greener, then plays the guitar:
Laialy El Shemal El Hazeena*, yes "Sad Northern Nights"* my fear came vital, and the door closed.
 I imagine my friends whispering innocent love stories while we were preparing a Syrian breakfast Fattah*:
-Are you still waiting for me? How long, my dear?!
-My daughter reminds me of you; she moves her hands just like you do when talking.
-Every time I cry, I remember you; what would happen if you were here?
My grandmother:
-Stand your ground only when you want it to be your ground.
My aunt smokes in the garden driveway:
 - I will not quit smoking. So, could you not advise me, Doctor?
My cousins design a wedding dress:
- Do you remember you taught us when we were kids to play "Beit Peyot"*?

161

And from the big windows, Ali's drawings look at me and fill the place. Drawings unite the Alawite blood, Sunni, Druze, Shiite, Kurdish, Yazidi, Christian, Jewish, Amazigh, and every attribute created by humans and partisan within it.

All "bloods" are the same for all who knew love.

-Hope does not reside in baskets but in "times."

-The only solution is for women to rule us; the men's opportunity is over, and they failed.

I look at the ceiling; I see the sky.

My house is without a roof; the sky is its limitation and mine!

My house is without a ceiling; it is not disturbed by geography, it is not burdened by history, and all religions protect it with no exception.

My stairs are from and to the sky. They are made of nettles from all countries, from the ocean of gas to the Gulf of Petroleum.

And the sky is filled with groups of (Tuk-Tuk) with young people shouting, "We want a homeland."

Sky of warm hands bandaging the wounded, children planting roses, mothers distributing food in tents without a homeland.

The sky resounds with the crying of the bereaved. It trembles with the hypocritical strict religious groups' claps.

And in moments of silence before the storm, the voices of the expatriates chirped:

-We miss you.

The sky becomes a mirror of revolutions needed by the countries of the first alphabet and the first civilizations, weeping and longing farewell to loved ones, and the collapse of systems and regimes.

-Where are you, God? If you do exist, help us.

Save us from those who speak on your behalf and those who made them.

I looked at the hummingbird; it was all in one color, blue, the color of the sky.

-"My hope lives in you. I love you".

I sewed the last jacket and threw it over another swan's story; thus, "you were vowed to the sun. "

The stairs of nettles in the house got longer, and God shone in the sky.

162

To Be Continued...

Explanation:

-Ahl al-Bayt*: 'People of the House": Refers to the family of the Islamic prophet Muhammad

- "Y' Jabal Albaeed" *: A beautiful Arabic song by the famous Arab icon Fairuz.

- Hareem*: It is an Arabic word that is sometimes used to describe washed-brain females that consider themselves males' belongings.

-Gaim*: An Arabic name that means white clouds.

- Ghadi*: An Arabic name that means "my tomorrow."

- Haram*: forbidden or proscribed by Islamic law.

-Better to have your enemy inside the tent pissing out than outside the tent pissing in." *
Original for US President Lyndon Johnson, regarding FBI Director J. Edgar Hoover, as quoted in The New York Times (31 October 1971).

- Tannour bread*: The name of famous bread baked in a clay oven in Syria and countries besides. It is very similar to tandoor bread.

- Milk Al-Yameen: * Sex slavery which ISIS tries to re-establish based on forger history. The words mean literally: The belongings of the right hand.

- Zoroastrianism*: A monotheistic pre-Islamic religion of ancient Persia founded by Zoroaster in the 6th century BC.

-Lady Zaynab*: Sayyida Zainab: The grandchild of Prophet Muhammad, the eldest daughter of Ali ibn Abi Talib. She is considered a figure of sacrifice, strength, and honesty for women in Islam.

-Zaynab* flowers: There are some white flowers commonly referred to as Zaynab flowers in some Arab countries.

- Alia, the Highest*:
The name Alia in Arabic means strong above silly things in life and high -in metaphor-so, the novel hero added the highest.
- Y': Ya*: Arabic vocative word, in English, it is a nonstandard spelling of you.

- Sexual jihad* (Arabic: jihad al-nikah): In brief: An unhuman style of "marriage" found by ISIS.
Per Wikipedia:
"It refers to the alleged practice in which women sympathetic to Salafi jihadism travel to war zones such as Syria and voluntarily offer themselves to be "married" to jihadist militants. Repeatedly and in temporary marriages, serving sexual comfort roles to help boost the fighters' morale.".

- Arabic coffee readings*A typical middle eastern tradition done by friends in the mornings as casual fortune-telling.

- Imam Ali*: Ali ibn Abi Talib:
He was the fourth Rashidun caliph, famous for his wisdom, cousin, son-in-law, and companion of Muhammad's Islamic prophet.
Per Wikipedia: Ali is one of the central figures in Shia Islam as the first Shia Imam and Sunni Islam as the fourth of the "rightly guided" caliphs.

-Zabiba*: A prayer callus: Is a callus on the forehead present in some "devout praying" Muslims from repeated prostration in prayer.

- Nigma*: An Arabic name that means a Star.

- Sabah*: An Arabic name that means the Morning.

- Zakat* is a form of almsgiving. It is considered in Islam a religious obligation.

- Do not ask me where you are from in Syria*: After the Syrian civil war, some people started to ask Syrians "from where in Syria" in a manipulating way to know the Muslim sects and make assumptions about a person's political orientation.

-May God strengthens your vulnerability*: A common Syrian expression said with gratitude.

-Syria, The Jasmine*: One of Syria's most used names by poets and writers, it came from the fact that Jasmine (Yasmine) is very common and widespread in Syria.

- Halal and Haram*: Common words in Arabic culture.
Halal is the Arabic word that means permitted. The opposite of halal is haram, meaning forbidden.

- Sero? What? What did you say? Do you mean I have to walk*? Sero pronunciation as an Arabic word means to walk.

- Sheikh*: A common word used to describe an Arab Muslim leader, the head of an Arab tribe or community when the leadership qualities came from a religious background.

-Zenobia* was a third-century queen of the Palmyrene Empire in Syria. She ruled a multicultural, multiethnic empire. Her story has inspired many artists and authors; she is a patriotic symbol in Syria.

- Superego*: According to Freud's psychoanalytic theory:
The "superego"* is part of the mind operates as a moral conscience.

The "id"* is the instinctual part of the mind that contains aggressive, forbidden, hidden memories and drives.

-Freekeh* is a famous Syrian dish; it is made from green wheat that is roasted and rubbed to create its flavor.

-Tahrir Square*: Liberation Square: A place located in Baghdad- Iraq.

-Laialy El Shemal El Hazeena*: Means "Sad Northern Nights"*: A famous Arabic song by Arabic icon Fairuz.

-Fatteh*: A middle eastern dish consisting of pieces of flatbread covered with a mixture of plain yogurt, boiled chickpeas, cumin, salt, lemon juice, and olive oil and topped with parsley, fried nuts, and pomegranate. Commonly it is eaten at breakfast or brunch.

-"Beit Peyot"*: Means: House and houses: A traditional Arabic children's game when children pretend they are in real life in the way they want and imagine daily living scenarios.

About The Author:

Lama Muhammad was born in Syria on November 24, 1979.
She spent her childhood in several countries, and the amount of
knowledge of different cultures accompanied her life and her writings.
She obtained her medical degree from Tishreen University in 2004,
graduating at the top of her class. She then completed a transitional year
in plastic surgery, burns, pediatrics, and internal medicine, followed by a
residency in dermatology and venereal disease at Damascus University
in 2008. After that, she practiced as a board-certified dermatologist in
Syria before emigrating to the United States.
She completed a preliminary year in internal medicine at Case Western
Reserve University, St. Vincent Charity Medical Center, before
matching at the University of New Mexico in general adult psychiatry.
She was Chief Resident in Psychiatry at the University of New Mexico
Health Sciences Center. She graduated with Diana Quinn Award for
service, compassion, and dancing healer spirit and Medical Students'
teaching award. Then she finished a Fellowship in Consultation-Liaison
(Psychosomatic)Psychiatry from the University of New Mexico.
Currently, Dr. Muhammad is an Assistant Professor of Psychiatry,
Double American Board-Certified in Psychiatry and Neurology, and in
Consultation Liaison/Psychosomatic Medicine Doctor at the University
of California in San Diego UCSD.
She started writing in the virtual space on secular websites in 2009.
After that, she continued writing and publishing her books through
various Arab and international publishing houses.
In addition to the weekly articles, the author has eight other books.
She introduces herself on her website, saying:

"I introduce myself and speak with you as a human being; I don't judge you by religion, color, gender, or nationality.

I care about whether you use your brain or not. Does the voice of your loved ones beat in your heart when your interest knocks on the door?!

If so, is there a dwarf place in the crowd of your comrades for me and my words?"

My name is Lama; in Arabic means the gentle wind, the breeze, and titles mean nothing to me.

I believe in love and humanity, in our ability to start from zero again and again!

We are all the same; only two things make us different: how we treat others and our dreams.

Medicine is my profession; writing is my sanctuary and my way of trying to contribute to a better tomorrow.

Before you clash with my thoughts and my beliefs, please visit my page and get to know me:

https://www.lamamuhammad.com

Please note:

My virtual house has no place for any religious or nationalist fanatic. There is no place for those who classify people by belonging to a sect.

My house is not for the praise and worship of idols, nor is it for treason or insulting any human being. If you want to invalidate a word, discuss it and refute it, every insult to its owner is unreliable defamation.

Suppose you cannot accept a woman who rises above the common to what the brain and the heart suggest, then do not venture into my house and my life.".
Lama Muhammad

The War's Kite And The Immigration's Key:
"Her Name is Muhammad"